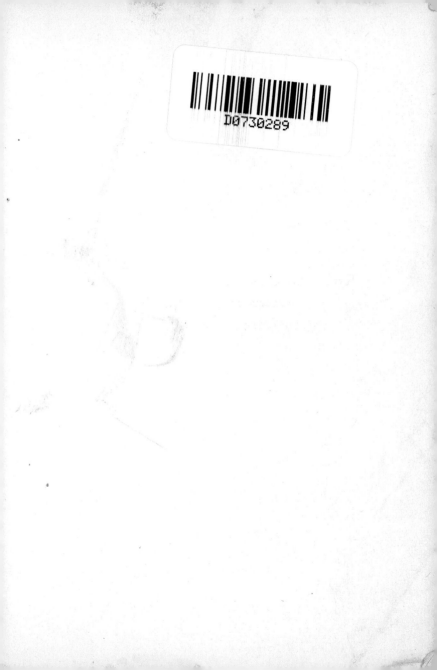

Your
Dreams

Your Dreams

Spiritual Messages in Pajamas

ANA LORA GARRARD

Llewellyn Publications
Woodbury, Minnesota

First Edition
First Printing, 2010

Cover art: background © YouWorkForThem, Inc.; flower © DigitalVision
Cover design by Ellen Dahl

Llewellyn Publications is a registered trademark of Llewellyn Worldwide Ltd.

Library of Congress Cataloging-in-Publication Data (Pending).
ISBN: 978-0-7387-2177-4

Llewellyn Publications
A Division of Llewellyn Worldwide Ltd.
2143 Woodale Drive
Woodbury, MN 55125-2989
www.llewellyn.com

Printed in the United States of America

Your Dreams: Spiritual Messages in Pajamas

Welcome dear reader. I'm so happy you're here. I invite you to treat this book as a meeting ground—a place where I can share insights I've cultivated over the years and you can receive recognition for the tremendous amount of knowledge within you.

I believe there is a quiet and potent wisdom that flows through the veins of each of us. Yet, whenever we narrow our thoughts because of fear, doubt ourselves because of old wounds, or allow ourselves to get distracted by our daily bustle, we shut off our ability to perceive much of the powerful awareness we carry within.

This book can help. Within its pages you will find some general information to help you identify what inner wisdom looks and feels like, how it gets choked off, and how it flows through a number of different channels, including your dreams. You will discover heart-centered tools for uncovering the wisdom within both your dreams and everyday life experiences that will allow you to gain new insights into who you are and what is really going on in your life. You will also get all the information you need to assemble a strong, supportive dream group.

For over twenty-five years, I've used the information in these pages to uncover the knowledge revealed within both my sleeping dreams and my waking experiences, which I call "waking dreams." I have taught others to do the same. As a direct result, many of my students and I have acquired new skills, made positive changes in our work and relationships, moved into new abodes, healed the sore spots in our hearts, opened new lines of communication with loved ones who died, stepped out of some dark pits of despair, had unexpected fun, and, perhaps most importantly, learned to comprehend ourselves and our purpose here on earth in very profound ways. In other words, we've used our dream explorations to create more rewarding lives for ourselves. I encourage you now to do this, too. Use the information here as a springboard to move further into your own native wisdom and invent a life for yourself that is filled with richness and creativity on every level.

Please remember that this book is intended as a guide and a source of inspiration. It is not a tome of ultimate truth. Although I frequently speak with a voice of authority, I encourage you to embrace only those concepts that resonate with you and to toss the rest out the window. I would be delighted if some of what I have learned in my journey may be of service to you in yours.

"Namaste," as the Hindus say. (The sparkling light within me honors the sparkling light within you.)

CONTENTS

PART TWO
Heart-centered Dream Exploration Tools

PART THREE
The Waking Dream

PART FOUR
The Dream Circle

Why This Book?

I am offering you this book for several reasons.

First of all, I would like to help you recognize that your inner wisdom is as real as the four walls that surround your body or this book you are holding in your hands. I'd like to help you discover all you can about your ability to inspire healing, create deeply fulfilling relationships, uncover immensely joyful work, make all the money you need, and face all the challenges before you in a creative, loving, and even humorous manner. In other words, I'd like to assist you in realizing all those things you know, but may not know you know.

Secondly, I want to encourage you to reclaim your dreams as channels for finding your own inner wisdom.

Remember that even though they might confuse your rational mind at times, your dreams do not belong to well-educated professionals, clairvoyant seers, or even brilliant dream book authors. They are yours. You don't need to push them aside or hand them over to someone else. You just need to learn to approach them outside the filter of your rational mind. Dreaming is a natural way that the wise being within you, your spirit, guides you through life. Because dreams come from within, you have all the insight-fulness and clairvoyance you need to understand them. By learning to use a few simple tools, you can reawaken your ability to comprehend them.

Thirdly, I want to invite you to expand your definition of the word "dream," so that you can explore your daily life as if it too is a dream. With the information provided in these pages, I seek to show you how to look below the surface of anything that's going on in your life, discover why you're having this experience, and uncover what it has to teach you about enriching your life path.

Lastly, I am writing this book because I wish to introduce you to a conscious, heart-centered approach to dream exploration that does not rely primarily on using your brain. By this I mean that instead of using intellectual analysis as a means of comprehending what's going on in your dreams and waking life, I want to guide you through the process of feeling what you know inside so that you can understand all your experiences in a more profound manner. An amazing thing happens when you probe the underlying layers of both your sleeping and waking experiences in this way. You enter into direct contact with the wise, old being within you who knows how to bring new levels of love and healing into your time on earth. In other words, you begin to discover the compassionate healer, teacher, therapist, spiritual warrior, and psychic channel that dwell within you.

I can think of nothing I would rather share with you.

HOW TO USE THIS BOOK

Before I explain how to use this book, let me explain how the material in these pages is laid out. This book is divided into four parts. Part One answers questions about inner wisdom, dreams, and how your soul uses dreams to guide you.

Part Two presents tools for conscious, heart-centered dream exploration that can help you comprehend the insights your soul is offering you through different dreams. It includes examples of ways different individuals have used these tools so you can see how they work.

Part Three provides ideas for exploring your life as a waking dream. The ideas you will find here are especially useful when you feel frustrated, upset, or curious about something that is going on in your waking hours. By assisting you in taking a deeper look at your everyday life experiences, the tools can help you understand them and respond to them more fully. This section includes a large number of examples that give you a picture of how the ideas I've presented work for different people.

Part Four offers all the information you need to create an inspiring, supportive dream circle. It shows you how a committed group of people can explore their dreams and/or waking life experiences together on a meaningful level.

How you use this material depends on what you'd like to get out of it. If you'd just like to learn more about dreams and inner wisdom and how these two parts of your experience work together, I suggest reading all of Part One and the exercise examples given in Part Two and Part Three. If you'd like to start remembering your dreams more often, carefully read over Chapter Three, "Remembering Your Dreams." And if you're ready to learn something new from your dreams and/or your waking experiences, read all of Parts One, Two, and Three. Then use some of the tools you find there to work with a dream or waking experience of your choice. To explore a dream, return to Chapter Eight in Part Two called "How to Start Exploring." To explore a waking life experience, turn to the section in Part Three called, "A Quick Guide to Using Waking Dream Exercises" and begin there. If you decide to explore your dreams as part of a group and would like specific information to help you get going, read Part Four.

No matter how you choose to work with this book, remember that you can have fun while you're doing it. Browse through the ideas presented here. Use them in your own way. Dream. Scribble away. Dream some more. Let your own secret wisdom rise to the surface of your awareness.

PART ONE

Questions
and Answers

CHAPTER ONE

The Wisdom within You

WHAT IS INNER WISDOM?

If you cracked yourself open like a walnut, you'd find a part of yourself that knows things. That's your inner wisdom. It's a profoundly creative and healing aspect of your being that you may not realize is there, but it is.

Because this part of you has never believed what you've been told about yourself, or reality that wasn't or isn't true, it doesn't get misled by worries, fears, and incomplete information. Even though other parts of yourself may have fallen asleep or succumbed to numbness or injury, your inner wisdom has stayed awake, whole, and alert. It sees your experience at the moment for what it truly is, and your inner wisdom tries to help your everyday self see more clearly, too.

Since it perceives no solid boundaries between you and anything else in your experience, this aspect of yourself can, at any time, draw on the wisdom of what I call "the rest of the cosmos." It can absorb knowledge from trees, rocks, and stars; it can also talk to faraway people and spirits from other realms.

In the most loving way possible, this part of your being constantly encourages you to open up to yourself, to relationship, to life, to joy, and to All That Is. It invites you to embody all that you truly are. It is you in your most essential form.

WHAT DOES INNER WISDOM
LOOK LIKE IN EVERYDAY LIFE?

Most of us dance back and forth between forgetting and remembering our inner wisdom hundreds of times each day. When we forget our inner wisdom for brief periods, we react to people and situations with inattention, confusion, or fear. We stop breathing fully, clench up our muscles, feel small, weak, dizzy, or defective. We lose track of what we feel and topple into thoughts of scarcity, struggle, and judgment. Or we stomp around, taking some miniature idea of who we are far too seriously.

Conversely, when we remember our inner wisdom for short spells of time, we respond to people and situations with love, clarity, and presence. We invite ourselves to breathe deeply, feel gratitude for all the crazy miracles in our lives, and see our own individual sparkle. We also begin to set clearer intentions, communicate as openly and sensitively as we can with all the other amazing beings we meet, and remind ourselves of what's important in life.

Though most of us make lots of quick little shifts throughout each day between these two polar ways of being, we may also go through different phases in our lives when we envelop ourselves in one way of being or the other.

If we forget the truths we know deep inside on a long-term basis, we usually start feeling worried, stressed, depressed, bored, dull, lonely, or isolated. We experience aches, pains, and illness in our bodies. We become highly self-critical or begin telling ourselves that we can only survive by struggling. Our sense of humor becomes cracked and rusty, causing us to drop into a big, black hole of despair. We lose our ability to glimpse any of the glimmering constellations that lie within our own hearts.

On the other hand, when we remember how to stay connected to the warmth and inspiration within our own spirits for longer periods, we begin to notice an overall

softening in our lives. We start allowing ourselves to cel-
ebrate our own beauty. We experience more love seeping
in from all quarters. Moments arise when we feel deeply
linked to all the multi-faceted individuals that surround us.
Our own spiritual guidance grows clearer, as we allow our
minds to open to new, mind-bending possibilities.

During our adult lives, many of us make an overall shift
in the direction of embracing our spirit's wisdom more and
more strongly. Once we decide to open to our own growth,
we spend less time forgetting and more time remembering
all the amazing truths that we know. Yet, we may still feel
very stuck at moments.

WHY CAN'T I FEEL MY INNER WISDOM?

Though your inner wisdom is vital and you need to be in
touch with it to grow and feel happy, you may still have difficulty sensing it at times. When you shift your underlying
focus to your wounds and disappointments and to thoughts
of fear and self-denial, you effectively shut the door to the
things that you, in a less defended state, know are real. You
have to open your mind at least a tiny crack to new possibilities if your own sacred truths are to shine through.

Most likely, when you were a child, you opened to what
you knew naturally. You could feel there was something in-

credibly precious inside of you. Though you probably didn't give words to it like "inner wisdom," you sensed that you were full of beauty, magic, and a thousand unopened gifts. Yet because of what you learned from your family, friends, teachers, acquaintances, and society-at-large, you began to lose touch with this inherent knowing at a very early age. In its place you adopted some very limited ideas about what you and the world were capable of. You may have begun to think that there was something wrong with you. Maybe you took on the thought that you weren't good, you weren't lovable, or you weren't kind, smart, capable, creative, generous, or responsible. Perhaps you started to believe that the world was an unfriendly place and that you had to concentrate hard on avoiding certain things in order to stay safe.

Pushing aside the truths that pulsed in your veins, you listened to what other important people in your life were telling you about what was real. You learned to distrust your inner impulses. You unconsciously allowed others' limited ideas to be imprinted in your mind and subtly shape your life. If something went wrong in your experience, you assumed it was because of some sloppiness in your thinking rather than because you had separated yourself from your own inner wisdom. Now you may not feel even the teeniest hope that your inner wisdom is alive within you, but it is.

HOW DO I GET BACK IN TOUCH
WITH WHAT I KNOW?

Even though you sometimes break away from what you know, from what feels right to you, the wise part of you doesn't disappear. Despite the fact that you may fall into confusion and despair for long periods, it doesn't go away. You just stop noticing its presence.

You see, your wisdom isn't a passive thing. Instead, it's like a powerful river that keeps flowing forward at all times. It is a force. It's a vibrant energy within you that keeps urging you to grow and open up to it in every way possible. You couldn't get away from it if you wanted to. It keeps trying to make contact with you, keeps trying to slip into your awareness, even when you're not paying attention. And like most powerful rivers, it courses down a number of different channels.

Sometimes your inner wisdom shows up as that little voice in your head that tells you things like "slow down," "breathe deeply," "eat this," "turn here," or "listen to him before you bite his head off." Sometimes it comes in as a big voice that says, "this is ultimately the kind of work I want to do in my life" or "this is the kind of relationship I want to invest in." Sometimes it shows up in the form of intuition, flashes of creative inspiration, and strong sensations of either imbalance and tension or balance and vitality in your body. And sometimes it gets reflected in the events that are taking place around you. (See Part Three for more information about this.)

You don't have to excavate your inner wisdom with a lot of sweat and hard work. You don't have to spend years immersing yourself in a strict meditative practice or receiving the tutelage of some ascended master in order to make contact with it. You just need to allow it in. It is flooding the very spot where you are sitting at this moment. It's in your ears, cheeks, and nostrils. It's in your left elbow and your right knee. If you breathe deeply, gently relax your mind, and listen with your whole heart, you can begin to sense it.

Of course, you can also feel your inner wisdom strongly by listening to your dreams. That's what we'll talk about next.

CHAPTER TWO

How "Sleeping Dreams" Reveal Inner Wisdom

WHAT DO DREAMS HAVE TO DO WITH INNER WISDOM?

Dreams come from the wise part of you that has the ability to cast a far-reaching and loving gaze into the heart of all things. They illuminate the wide, gentle truths that you know are real. They help you to see that life is more than you sometimes think it is, and that you are more than you think you are.

Your dreams remind you that you are not defined by your family, your career, or the amount of money you have nestled away in a bank. Likewise, you are not defined by the color of your skin, the shape of your body, or the number of years you have tromped around on this planet. In other words, you are neither your physical circumstances nor your own limited thoughts. The physical details of your life and the thoughts you hold are merely pieces of your human journey. Though these details and thoughts are part of you and they often have a beauty of their own, they do not tell the whole story of who you are.

You are greater than the sum of all your concrete, known experiences and beliefs. You are the softest turquoise and the deepest green. You are a rushing river, a soaring eagle, a howling coyote, you are strength, courage, and kindness itself, and many hidden friends love you.

The real you is pure poetry, pure creative possibility, and pure delight. The closer you come to realizing this, the closer you come to finding your heart's most treasured path. This is what your dreams keep telling you, so open your eyes wide.

You are so much more than you think you are.

WHAT HAPPENS WHEN I
FALL ASLEEP AND DREAM?

To fall asleep, as the word "fall" suggests, is to release control. When you drift off to sleep, you let go in many ways.

You quit holding onto all the limited thoughts that have been restricting your experience during your waking hours. You stop believing that you are your body, which is perhaps one of the most limited thoughts of all. Tumbling freely through time and space, you open yourself to the truth of what is going on in your human/spiritual existence.

As you do this, the wise, radiant aspect of who you are—your soul—is able to speak more clearly with you. It talks to you about things you have been afraid to look at, or have just been unable to see, while you are awake. Using colorful imagery, this part of you helps you to recognize both your self-imposed limitations and your own essential nature. It shows you how to solve problems in your life by expanding your thoughts about who you are and what is possible. Your soul invites you to consider what you need to do in order to get on a life path that truly makes your heart sing.

This is dreaming. It is something you sink into every night, and it is a gift. It is one of the means through which your own spirit reminds you that you can reshape your waking life by using the powerful awareness that lives within you.

HOW DO I BEGIN
TO UNDERSTAND MY DREAMS?

Deep understanding comes when you explore the feelings that a dream brings up in you. I have provided some tools in Part Two to help you do this.

Many of these tools ask you to call forth your own infinite compassion and experience one or more of your dream images as aspects of yourself. You can accomplish this either by pretending that you are the character you are focusing on and allowing this character to speak with you, or by immersing yourself in the essence of this character through movement and sound.

I recommend that you use a heart-centered approach if you wish to understand your dreams in the most profound manner. If you rely, instead, on dream dictionaries, psychologists, or even the microscope of your own intellect to assist you in "interpreting your dreams," you may miss the whole big wonder and excitement of what your dreams are actually telling you. You may end up with labels for the images but lack awareness deep in your bones of what your dreams are saying.

For example, suppose you had a dream about a barking dog. A dream dictionary or an "expert" might inform you that this dream has to do with setting personal boundaries. You may think to yourself that setting personal boundaries makes sense, but you may not really understand this dream much more completely than you did to begin with. Having this new descriptive phrase might placate that dear portion of your mind that wants to have an instant definition for your experiences, yet it wouldn't help you absorb the dream's meaning in a way that would have a strong impact on your life.

On the other hand, if you looked within and allowed yourself to feel that noisy dog inside yourself—recognizing what this dog is afraid of, what it's trying to protect, and what it loves (thereby remembering what you're afraid of, what you're trying to protect, and what you love)—then the message of this dream would become clearer and more real. The experience would change you, enlarge your own experience of yourself in a way that cannot be completely described in words. At the most elemental level, you would experience this fiercely protective dog as an energy that is rising within you. Then you could consciously decide how you would like to respond to that energy.

Dreams come from the warm, loving center of your soul. Asking what a dream means is the same as asking what the oldest, wisest part of your being wants you to remember at this moment. When you allow your dreams to lead you into a stronger realization of who you are and what you know in the very core of your being, you take the first step toward understanding your dreams in a meaningful way. The specific tools designed to help with dream understanding are the Point of View, Dialoguing, Dream Body, or Themes exercises in Part Two.

WHY DO I DREAM ABOUT CERTAIN IMAGES?

You are a vast, magnificent being who sometimes experiences complete amnesia about who you are. At the same time, your inner wisdom/soul/spirit does not forget your true nature. This part of you sends you messages in dream images. Each image you receive is designed to awaken you in some specific way so that you can remember more of your own real essence.

Sometimes a dream image directly mirrors one of your own limited thoughts so you can see just how painful and restrictive that thought is. For example, if you secretly believe you're a bad person and treat yourself in an incredibly critical manner, then you might dream about a big, scary man attacking you with a knife. After exploring this image you might find that it reflects the harmful way you've been treating yourself; it awakens you to the fear and pain you create by degrading yourself. Like a bright, flashing neon sign, this image of a scary, knife-wielding man catches your attention and signals you to treat yourself with more kindness and compassion.

At other times, dream images illuminate what your experience would be like without your limiting thoughts. For instance, if you've been thinking that you are incapable of manifesting any of your own cherished life goals, you might have a strong dream about a pilot confidently landing a plane. By exploring this pilot as a part of yourself after you awaken, and *feeling* what it is like to be a pilot something could shift within you. Whether for just one moment or for a longer period of time, some of the self-assurance the pilot feels could surge through you.

As a result of this dream, you might feel a small opening in your thoughts about who you are and what you are capable of doing. You might consider the possibility that you are actually able to guide some creation from the spirit plane to earth, just as the pilot did in your dream. You might even feel brave enough to follow up on some of your own wonderful inspirations you'd thought were too crazy to pursue.

Of course, you might not do any new things right away, but this simple dream could plant a new seed in your thoughts. It could help you to see yourself in a new way and encourage you to recognize that you are a capable creator.

Whenever you open your heart and mind to what lies below the surface of your dreams, you can see that each dream image is there to help you relax into another part of your own large being. Even a simple dream can help you challenge your own limiting thoughts and recognize what your life might be like if you didn't think that way. Dreams can usher you in to a new richer level of life experience.

WHY DO DREAMS SEEM SO CONFUSING?

Many of the rules that define reality, as we know it, disappear in dreams. Without our rational minds at the helm, directing our experience, time and space move freely, like rivers coursing down a mountain in springtime. Past, present, future, near and far all slide into one another like melting chunks of snow. Relationships blend into one another, too. The edges that divide different objects, animals, plants, and people all change or dissolve from one moment to the next.

In one dream, you may see your childhood swing set standing outside a sacred site you visited in India as an adult. In another dream, you may see a sleek otter diving for fish in a pool of water that's sitting in the middle of your workplace. This can be confusing. If a wise part of yourself is trying to communicate with you through dreams, you may wonder why it chooses to do so in such a befuddling way.

Your dreaming soul needs to speak to you in a symbolic language in order to teach you the immense truth of who you are. It casts its net widely through time and space, revealing information to you that cannot be described any other way.

Because your true reality, the totality of your experience as a spirit, is not bound by time or space, neither are your dreams. This mega-space and mega-time quality of dreams is the main reason why you feel baffled by them when you wake up. People are most comfortable dividing experiences into neat categories like past or present, real or imagined, here in the United States or over there in Asia. But your dreaming spirit doesn't hold to these tidy little ways of boxing up reality.

Instead, dreams are a very tangible way for your dreaming soul to remind you that all dimensions of experience are blended together in one great living sea of awareness. It plops down certain dream images side by side or mixes them together when these images are somehow linked together in your heart.

So, if you wish to understand the dream about the swing set at the sacred site you might begin by gently allowing yourself to relax into the memory of what it was like to swing on a swing set as a child. Can you imagine swinging with your hair and clothes flapping in the wind, with maybe some Band-Aids on your knees, and your sneakers shooting up toward the sky? Recall what that feels like. Allow yourself to be that kid. Then ask yourself, "What is it I know when I become a child and pump my legs into the air? Can this knowledge enhance what I learned while kneeling at that sacred site in India?" If you can feel the link between the happy-go-lucky swinging you did as a little kid and the divine place you sought to visit as a grown-up kid, you may be able to add a fresh perspective to your own spiritual quest.

Likewise, if you desire to comprehend the dream of the diving otter at your workplace, breathe deeply, let your edges dissolve, and feel what the otter knows as she curves through the water aiming for a fish. Can you feel the swooshing water around you, and your relaxed attentiveness as you/she dives? By allowing yourself to be the otter, and sense what she senses as she dives for her goal, you may start to understand how this creature's innate knowledge can transform a seemingly unrelated experience such as your work.

You see, your dreaming self knows that while you are a unique, sparkling individual, you are not separate from other people, or from wind, water, animals, and trees. Your childhood is not isolated from your present or your future. Steps you take today may be an echo of a time you walked on sun-baked Egyptian soil or on the surface of a glowing blue planet. At any moment, you can learn from other dimensions of your experience.

The part of you that sends you dreams—your soul—realizes the bigness of who you are. It recognizes your connection to all things and sees that you are a being of tremendous magnitude who is trying to embody the vastness of who you are during this human lifetime. So when your soul offers you guidance for your current waking life situation, it presents you with many-faceted dream images that not only provide information about your present experience, but which also remind you of your larger reality.

Now, as I said earlier, your mind may initially have trouble comprehending your dream messages because it has been trained to define your experience very narrowly. Yet your heart, which is the loving bridge between your human self and the Great Spirit that lives within everything, can still recognize what your soul is trying to communicate to you. By listening to your heart and feeling your dream images as parts of yourself, you can dissolve any confusion that arises in your mind when you first look at them.

With practice your mind can begin to embrace your own big, warm inner wisdom as fully as your heart does.

CHAPTER THREE

Remembering Your Dreams

WHY DON'T I
REMEMBER MY DREAMS?

To remember our dreams is a choice we make. It may be an unconscious choice, but it is still a choice. Many of us don't see value in our dreams, or we find them so bizarre that we unconsciously decide to let all memory of them dissolve, just as we forget all those sights and sounds in our daily lives that don't mean anything to us. Others of us choose, on some level, to ignore our dreams because something or someone demands our immediate attention first thing in the morning.

Though it is generally very easy for me to recall my dreams (after about thirty years of regular practice), there was a time when I consciously allowed my dreams to fade from my memory. My kids were little and I knew that I wanted to focus on them when they pushed their bright faces up against mine as soon as I woke up. So I just released my dreams to the ethers, and I was clear with myself that I was making a choice.

Yet, why do we forget our dreams when we think that we do want to recall them? There may be many reasons for this, but I am familiar with the following two.

Sometimes, we unwittingly close the doors to our dreams because we are secretly scared of what they might tell us. Either we are afraid to hear a specific message or we just have a general fear that dreams will dredge up something unpleasant from a dark and dreaded place in our beings. Because we do not yet trust the full sweetness of who we are, we keep our dreams at bay.

At other times, our dreams slip away because we neglect to hold an inviting place for them in our minds. If we fill our consciousness with habitual thoughts by dwelling on the past or mulling over plans for the day ahead as soon as we awaken, we leave little opportunity for dreams to make their presence known. Dreams quickly lose their visibility in a mind that is jam-packed with other ideas.

Remembering dreams entails cultivating openness within. It means allowing ourselves to breathe and be from the first moment we awaken. It means remaining for a while in a soft, receptive state so that our dreams have room to come in.

Again, recalling dreams is a choice. After we lay aside any fears about what our spirits might tell us and leave enough space in our minds to invite dreams in, they quickly come forward, like honored guests. Our dreams always become clearer when we welcome them in fully.

HOW CAN I REMEMBER MY DREAMS MORE CLEARLY?

Here are a few tips:

- Before you go to sleep, ask yourself if you agree to give yourself time and space to wake up, to breathe, feel your feelings, and honor your dreams. Allow yourself some relaxed time in the morning without catapulting immediately out of bed, combing worriedly through the past, or diving into a great sea of plans for the day. Be willing to be quiet and discover the wisdom that your dreams (and your soul) have to share with you. If you feel any uncertainty about your ability to do these things and you wish to recall your dreams, I invite you to take a moment and explore the source of your uncertainty. Gently consider what is really keeping you from arranging your life and your thoughts in ways that give you room to experience your dream world to a greater degree.

· Once you are ready to remember your dreams, I invite you to circle some positive thoughts through your mind—thoughts like: "I welcome my dreams into my life now" or "I believe in the enormous and persistent love that shapes my dreams" will help you to remember.

· Within easy reach of the place where you sleep, keep one of the following three items to help you anchor your dreams in the morning:

> · A dream journal and pen (if you'd like to write your dreams down)
> · A sketchbook and drawing implements (if you'd like to sketch images or feelings from your dreams)
> · A tape recorder with a microphone (if you'd rather tell your dreams out loud or sing about them)

· Right before you go to sleep, remind yourself that you are going to remember your dreams in the morning. Commit to giving yourself some relaxed, undefined time after you wake up that is uncluttered by your plans for the day.

· Optional Step. If you'd like your inner wisdom to address a specific question, write this question down before you doze off.

· After you wake up, allow yourself to remain in a peaceful, receptive state. Wait quietly for dream feelings and images to come floating through. Once you've remembered as many as you can while lying in one position, return to any other positions you know you were sleeping in to see if this jogs your memory of any different images.

· Record whatever images you've recalled in your dream journal, sketchbook, or on your tape recorder—even if you only got a few wisps. Sometimes recording one sliver of a dream can help spark your memory of other images, so make note of whatever comes through.

If you have limited time in the morning and can't record all the details of your dreams, write down a few key words that will help trigger your memory of the images. Then write them down later when you do have time. These shorthand notes might look something like: "drooping tree . . . woman with big ears feeling angry," or "laughing man . . .lots of orange bugs." Be sure to write down any feelings that were a part of each dream. This information will help you later if you choose to explore the meaning of the images.

If you asked a question of your dreams as you went to sleep the night before, assume that the images you have recorded contain the answers you need. Turn to the Dialoguing exercise in Part Two if you'd like to explore this answer further.

As you seek to remember your dreams, be infinitely patient with yourself. This is a new adventure—a whole new learning experience. Know that your ability to recall your dreams will keep blossoming with practice.

By being persistent but gentle with yourself, you will remember your dreams more clearly and lavishly all the time. Your spirit will use your dreams as a channel through which to speak with you if that is what you truly desire.

CHAPTER FOUR

———

Dreams as Part of You

ARE ALL MY DREAM
IMAGES PARTS OF ME?

Yes. Each dream image, as well as everything else in this universe, is part of who you are. You are intricately connected to all that exists. The more you ask how a dream image is a part of you, the more you learn about the different aspects of the universe that dwell within your own heart, and the more pieces of yourself you get to retrieve and heal.

Now, at first glance, you may not always be able to see the way in which a dream plant/animal/person/object/landscape reflects some portion of yourself. You may, however, encounter a dream character—e.g., a giant purple banana or a drooling old lady—that you don't want to believe has anything to do with you. But I encourage you to press on and open your heart to all your dream characters, even if they seem disgusting, scary, or really strange to you at the beginning. As you open your heart and acknowledge that a dream character is part of you, remember that it does not mean you and that character are the same or even similar, but that there is a shared spark between the two of you. That big colorful banana or sweet drooling old human being you dream about may actually have much more to tell you than you realize.

To find out what you and any dream character have in common, try immersing yourself in that character. Playfully pretend that you are he, she, or it, even if the character is an inanimate object, some sort of plant, or an entity like the ocean. Feel what this character feels, say what this character has to say, and move in the manner that this dream character moves. (Detailed descriptions of how to do this are included in Part Two.) Rather than judging your dream character, look for the spark the two of you share. Once you begin to explore your dream character in this fashion, your initial resistance generally dissolves.

By working with my dreams in this manner, I have found incredible wisdom and creativity available to me. My edges have softened and my judgments of others have largely melted away, and I feel an ever-deepening sense of unity and contentment within.

When we begin to awaken both to our own uniqueness and to our connection with all beings, we enter realms of almost unimaginable sweetness. Exploring any dream image, as an aspect of ourselves, is one powerful step we can take in this direction.

WHY DO I DREAM ABOUT PEOPLE, PLACES, AND SITUATIONS FROM MY PAST?

Your spirit uses your dreams to guide you in your growth as a human being. Each night it brings forth images that can give you insights into parts of yourself that are ready to shift, some of which come from your past.

For example, suppose you have a dream about your seventh-grade English teacher, a person who strongly applauded the fanciful stories you invented about fiery dragons, headstrong princesses, and restless kingdoms. Because she believed in your potential as a writer, this teacher might appear in your dreams now to help you reclaim your own belief in your creative abilities. If you did a dream exercise that allowed you to be this teacher and see yourself from her perspective, you might rekindle both your faith in your own gifts and your willingness to use those gifts.

On the other hand, suppose you dreamed about an uncle who verbally abused you when you were a child. This relative might turn up in a dream because, as an adult, you have internalized his harshness—you are often critical of yourself and expect only rough treatment from others. Having this sort of dream may help you to recognize the abrasive way in which you've been treating yourself. It might also inspire you to embark upon some sort of dream exploration, therapy, or other self-transformational work that would permit you to further illuminate the abusive uncle within and gently heal that part of yourself.

Any time you explore your dream images, whether they are from the past, present, or future, you allow some aspect of your personality to expand. Your vast, wise soul uses your dreams to show you parts of yourself that are ready to be loved into something bigger.

WHY DO SOME
DREAM IMAGES KEEP REPEATING?

I am aware of two main reasons that the same dream images keep coming back.

Sometimes, when you are not listening fully to yourself, or not understanding a message your spirit is sending, a certain dream scenario may be replayed until you do listen and you do understand. These dreams may seem nightmar-ish (if this is your experience I suggest you read the ques-tion about nightmares that follows this one) or they may just seem benign and insistent.

For example, suppose you are dreaming night after night about losing your keys, a child, or your sense of direction. By exploring these images, you might realize that you've been losing touch with something vital within yourself and forget-ting the reason that you are doing whatever you are doing in your life. Perhaps you need to slow down, breathe deeply, and consider what you truly intend to focus on. Once you start contemplating your real priorities in this way, then your soul no longer needs to send you messages about "losing some-thing important." Your repeating dreams about misplacing something can simply fade away.

Recurring dreams like the ones mentioned here try to draw your attention to a specific area of your life that needs your nurturing attention. They generally occur during a short time frame and quickly end when you get the mes-sage your spirit is transmitting.

However, powerful recurring dreams can also remind you of some essential aspect of yourself. These kinds of im-ages may keep reappearing over a long span of time. In these instances, you may dream over and over about a cherished childhood home or a much beloved activity from your past. Or you might keep encountering something mysterious—a sacred object, an animal, or a place you seem drawn to even though it is not one you've ever seen during your waking hours. In each case, the images affect you strongly either by putting you deeply at ease (if you feel ready to embrace more of who you are) or by making you extremely uncomfortable (if you feel that acknowledging the truth of who you are and what you feel is unsafe).

For example, I have dreamed about lionesses and lions since I was young. During childhood, I had nightmares of lionesses chasing me while I ran away screaming. At that time, those images scared me so badly I almost peed in my pajamas. As I grew older, however, my lion dreams shifted. Instead of feeling terrified of them, I gradually began to feel more curious. Then I started to experience a profound sense of awe and joy whenever I was in the presence of a lion or lioness and this allowed some new things to happen in my dreams. Once I reached out and touched a lion's soft fur, and once I became a roaring lioness with no memory of being human at all.

After exploring many of these dreams as an adult, I saw how their evolution mirrored my growing ability to embrace what was most natural to my being. The lionesses represented my own very intense desire to be wholly and freely "myself." They helped me recognize what it would feel like to live a life in which I did not hide or compromise unnecessarily, but instead went forward with commitment and confidence. When I was young, I felt I wouldn't be safe adopting this fierce degree of inner loyalty. But as I got older, I began to actively seek my own personal truths and devote myself to honoring them. The lion dreams reflected this overall shift.

Through time, I've noticed that my great dream felines reappear with a certain ferocity whenever I spend more than two seconds contemplating the possibility of making a major choice in my waking life that runs contrary to my own essential being. And they come back vibrating with an incredible strength that is not at all aggressive whenever I need to appreciate my authentic self more.

You too may have recurring dream images that act as dream totems to help guide you on your journey through life. If so, I highly encourage you to make note of these dream helpers and acknowledge them in some creative way. Try talking to them (use the Dialoguing exercise from Part Two), cut out photos and make collages about them, draw them, create poems in their honor, dance their movements, or sing songs that capture the essence of what the dream images mean to you.

At the same time, allow yourself to soak up everything these dream guides have to teach you about embracing your own unique potential. These images reflect some precious part of who you are and they appear time and again to lead you toward deeper self-love.

WHY DO I HAVE NIGHTMARES?

Deep down, our beings yearn to embody who we are more fully. If this forceful desire for growth keeps getting thwarted, the tension that results can cause nightmares.

Nightmares usually appear either when a wounded part of ourselves desperately needs healing, when we are obstinately resisting the winds of change, or when we are stuck in a pattern of pretending that we are small, weak creatures, (rather than acting as the powerful and infinitely creative beings that we are). Though the threats within them seem to come from someone or something outside our selves, frightening dreams are actually reflections of our own self-limiting attitudes and behaviors.

Scary dreams are a way that our souls use to grab our attention. They are high volume wake-up calls from our spirits that let us know it's time to listen.

Because nightmares show us very tangibly how much pain we cause our hearts and our bodies by not allowing ourselves to accept our own deepest wisdom, they may seem unnerving at first. Yet underneath the surface, nightmares contain empowering, life-affirming messages from a part of ourselves that loves us wholeheartedly. Whenever we open up enough to absorb these messages, our nightmares quickly vanish.

For example, suppose you dreamed of driving up a hill that kept getting steeper and steeper, making your car slip backward. Your first reaction might be to jerk yourself awake. But if you calm yourself down from the panicky feeling that woke you and remind yourself that the dream was trying to give you a strong message, you'd probably find the fear you experienced upon awakening begin to dissolve.

If you then explored this dream in an openhearted way instead of just pushing it aside, you most likely would feel the dream completely dissolve. So, instead of feeling at the mercy of some mean hill that wouldn't keep its shape, you might realize that the dream illustrated recent choices you have made to drive yourself unrelentingly toward some extremely difficult goals. You'd have the opportunity to consider why you push yourself so hard and what you could do to treat yourself more kindly.

Once you realize what your nightmares are telling you about changes you need to make in your thoughts and behaviors, they have served their purpose and do not need to return. You'll be done with them. Your soul will no longer need to use such dramatic images to remind you to treat yourself with greater gentleness.

Our souls want us to treat ourselves as kindly as possible. They want us to love, love, love ourselves. Whenever the subtler messages they send us about this are not getting through, they often resort to nightmares to get our attention. A nightmare's only purpose is to get us to listen to this voice of absolute tenderness within. As soon as we listen, all the darkness melts away.

To help your nightmares dissolve more easily, I recommend doing either the Dialoguing exercise in Chapter Seven, the Dream Body exercise in Chapter Eight, the Reworking exercise in Chapter Nine, or any combination of these. Be sure to ask a friend or a compassionate healer to assist you in this if you need the support.

CHAPTER FIVE

Dreams and Relationships

IS A DREAM ABOUT SOMEONE I KNOW IN WAKING LIFE A MESSAGE ABOUT A REAL PERSON?

Yes, it is, in a symbolic sense. It is also a message for you. Dreams very masterfully communicate on more than one level.

You dream about someone you know when an experience that is, has been, or will be a part of that other person's life has something to teach you. Such a dream indicates that the two of you are sharing life lessons in some way; your soul paths are overlapping. Remember, however, that the messages in dreams are metaphorical. A dream that a friend of yours is going to be in a train wreck may not be a warning that either you or your friend is going to be involved in an actual physical train wreck. Rather, it might be a message that both you and this person may be headed toward some big, wrenching challenges in the near future if you don't alter your thoughts and behaviors.

To unfold the meaning of this kind of dream I suggest you begin by feeling the person—this dream character you recognize from waking life—as a part of yourself. Ask them the questions given in the Dialoguing exercise in Part Two of this book. You could also use questions to learn about what this dream can tell you about this person's experience in waking life. In this way, you are able to see both the places where you and this other person come together on your spiritual journeys and the places where you move apart on your own individual treks through the cosmos.

Once I dreamt that the sadness a friend felt in her love life was causing a serious illness to build up in her uterus. I was worried for her when I woke up. I gradually realized this dream was a strong signal to me to make changes with my lover; it reflected the fact that I had not been feeling all that happy in my own relationship with my partner for a while. I sensed that my dreaming spirit was warning me that if I did not respond to my own rumbling feelings of distress, those pent-up emotions might cause me to experience some sort of strong physical trauma that I did not want. So after wrestling a couple more months with the part of me that did not want to let go, I finally decided to separate from my lover.

Despite the difficulty of this separation, I could feel in my gut that this was the path I needed to follow. Though often I felt sad about leaving my partner, a steady sense of serenity also began to grow in me as time went by, and I continued to be blessed by a healthy womb. My friend, however, ignored the tremors in her own love life and two years later had to have an operation to remove her uterus. My heart went out to her when this came to pass. As my dreams showed me, the two of us had stood at the same crossroads. Yet she had chosen to take the path to the left and I had chosen the one to the right. I felt a great deal of empathy for her.

Every dream, even one about a person you know, is an invitation to cast a soft, revealing light on another hidden valley within yourself. The more you can recognize what is going on inside of you, the easier it is to comprehend what is going on with others. As your self-awareness grows, so will your compassion.

WHY DO I HAVE ROMANTIC DREAMS?

Ah, romantic dreams—whether they contain intense, tantalizing sex or an amazing tender connection with someone who resonates deeply with you—all hold messages about love. Sometimes, however, the messages are not what you might think.

In a romantic dream, a character invites you to be more fully alive and more fully yourself. If you have great sex with this character, you might note upon awakening that the incredible physical release you experienced in the dream is helping you to relax more profoundly into your body. If you share a strong flow of affection, you might feel after you wake up as though your heart is more open. And if you just experience a very intense attraction in the dream, you may realize upon waking that this character's presence reminds you of some quality you'd like to develop within yourself.

In any event, waking up from a romantic dream isn't always easy. Believe me, I know. I spent many years as a single woman and often longed for an intimate partner. During this period I dreamt of six very adept, tall, dark-skinned men who were all making love to me at once. I also dreamed about a huge bear that loved me deeply. (Cross-species romance!) And I had many other dreams in which a dear, strong, gentle, and attractive man returned my affection very sweetly. Every time I awakened from one of these dreams, I felt crestfallen to return to a world in which I had not experienced such outpourings of tender appreciation.

After waking up many times from these romantic dreams, I finally learned to tell myself, with the utmost gentleness, that whatever I longed to receive from a loving dream character was something that also existed within myself. I reminded myself that this dream character simply echoed an unexplored aspect of the loving life force that poured through me.

I also taught myself to clarify what part of me this dream lover reflected by closing my eyes, breathing deeply, and asking the character questions such as: What part of me are you teasing into awakening? What do you have to show me about my innermost desires? What can I learn from you about loving myself? What do I need to do in order to experience you on the outside as well as the inside? What do you have to teach me about bringing romance into my waking life?

You can reassure yourself in the same way, by using this kind of dream exploration, to turn a romantic dream into an opportunity to know and love yourself more deeply. Discover how some precious part (or parts) of yourself most want to be embraced right now. Doing this might not make your longing for a special relationship go away, but it can help you to gain clarity, invite peace into your heart, and strengthen any present or future love relationships you may have on the physical plane.

Although a romantic dream may be an indication of an upcoming love affair with another person, if that is something you seek to create in your waking life, I suggest that you do not limit yourself by thinking of this kind of dream as a prophecy of something specific that may happen in your external world. Instead, try viewing your dream lover as a messenger from the powerful river of love that flows through you. Know that once you begin to cherish yourself and honor the truth of what you need and what you have to give, then love can come forth from many directions and fill your heart softly at every moment.

WHY DO I DREAM ABOUT PEOPLE WHO ANNOY ME IN WAKING LIFE?

We usually dream about someone who irritates us because this person has a powerful secret to reveal to us about ourselves.

A long time ago I worked as an activity director at a center for elderly people. For some reason that I couldn't quite put my finger on, one of my coworkers and I often had great difficulty cooperating with one another. She annoyed me. I thought we were as different as two people could be.

Then one night I dreamt about this coworker. Though the details of this dream seemed fuzzy upon awakening, I felt so uncomfortable dreaming about this woman that I decided to speak to her as a dream character and try to understand her more fully. I asked questions such as: What do you have to teach me? Why do you do that thing that particularly bugs me? What part of me do you represent?

I listened as quietly as I could to her answers and was surprised to discover that underneath the apparent contrasts between us, our intentions were very much the same. This floored me, because at that time in my life I very much believed in black and white divisions between myself and other people. I was sure that if I felt irritated by someone it was because they had a completely different Zip Code from mine—on the opposite side of the galaxy!

Yet my dreams indicated that this coworker and I were more similar than I'd realized. We both cared immensely for the people with whom we worked. In our own unique ways, we each sought to bring gifts of joy to people who needed it, and we both stretched ourselves in order to keep giving these gifts. All of this came as a revelation to me.

I had an even greater surprise when I returned to work and found that the tension between the two of us was gone. We had moved to a new level of mutual appreciation. I felt as if my dream exploration had miraculously opened both our hearts, because suddenly we could see each other for who we really were. Both our differences and our resistance to these differences had faded into the background.

In my experience, discomfort and resistance dominate our interactions with others for two main reasons. Either we persist in seeing others as less than they are or we fear their judgment so much that we portray ourselves as less than we are in their presence. The relationship denies either their star-filled magnitude or our own (and sometimes both).

To mend this kind of relationship, we can broaden the mental pictures that we hold of others and ourselves, and exploring our dreams can assist us with this. It helps us move beyond illusion so that the true elegance of others and ourselves becomes apparent.

CAN I COMMUNICATE WITH OTHER PEOPLE
THROUGH MY DREAMS?

Yes. All barriers to free-flowing communication disappear in dreams. When two spirits wish to make contact with one another, feelings can be shared in the dream state, even without any words being used. You can spot these direct messages from another's spirit by their strong vibratory quality.

While moments of clear connection with other people in dreams can be profoundly touching, you might want to remember that any dream message you receive from another person comes from that person's soul, not from his or her conscious mind.

This can be especially frustrating when you dream of receiving affection from a person who is important in your life but does not usually express love to you. Though this person's spirit may be able to recognize the love you share while in the dream state, his or her conscious, awake-self may not be able to acknowledge your connection.

For instance, when I was much younger I used to argue a lot with my grandmother. She could not seem to wrap her mind around the idea that I felt differently than she did about some things, or that I had chosen a life path that was very different from her path. Because I was a young woman at the time, her lack of acceptance shook my self-esteem to the core.

Then one night I dreamt that I was standing in a quiet gray space with her, near a fallen tree. I felt how important it was to her that I know, beyond a shadow of a doubt, how much she loved me.

The next time I visited my grandmother her behavior toward me had not substantially changed. She still belittled my choices and trampled over my fragile aspirations that I had forgotten to tuck out of view. However, because of the dream, I knew that down in the center of her very stubborn being `she did love me, and this new awareness helped me feel less rattled by her silly behavior. At moments, I saw very clearly how much our temporary struggles were dwarfed by the real love we shared.

As was the case with my grandmother, some people who open their hearts fully to you in dreams may do so only in that sphere. If this is the situation with someone you know and love on the physical plane, you may need to honor their choices and remind yourself that you do share boundless love in another realm.

However, you may receive dream messages from people who are open to sharing love and affection with you in the physical world as well as the dream state. In such instances, letting these people know that the two of you communicate on a spirit-to-spirit level in your dreams can often elevate your relationship. Sharing such dreams can remind you both of the many different dimensions in which your relationship is taking place and help you appreciate more fully the magic that has brought you into each other's lives.

WHY DO I DREAM ABOUT A LOVED ONE WHO DIED?

People who play a precious role in your life always remain part of the intricate fabric of who you are. The colorful threads of their beings stay woven into your awareness long after their bodies are gone. Often you dream about these souls simply to contemplate what they have shared with you during your time together.

Sometimes, however, your dreams become channels of direct contact with those who have passed beyond this plane. These dreams are distinctly different from other kinds of dreams in that they have an especially vivid quality that markedly affects your heart. If you listen to your own intuition, you will recognize this type of dream right away. In these instances, you have allowed the illusion of separation to dissolve so that a loved one who has left the earth can speak with you once again.

I experienced this myself a year after my father died. I dreamt I was sitting on the floor painting a picture when my father came over and said in a kind voice, "I didn't pay enough attention to you when you were little and I'm sorry."

As I looked up at my father, all the years of frustration and disappointment I had known with him rose up in one great rush and melted away. In the total silence that followed, I said, "I know. It's okay. I love you Dad." And for the first time in my awareness, it was okay. Then my father smiled at me and turned to go out the door. Before he disappeared, he transformed into a young Asian man.

I woke up gently from the dream, and my heart felt bathed in waves of tranquility. I was deeply grateful to have completed something with my father in the dream state that we did not have the capacity to complete while he was living.

During the last phase of my father's life, when he was dying of cancer, I was still a young woman, and I often felt a little intimidated by him. His first answer to every question I asked him seemed to be no. At that time, neither he nor I felt brave enough or wise enough to reach beyond that no to build the new bridges that could unite us more strongly. Through my dreams, however, I was able to experience forgiveness and healing that were not available to me during his time on earth. Everything changed in one instant of pure contact. From that time on, I have been able to love my father with no reservations.

Relationships do not need to end when physical life ends. When we leave the doors open, we can see that love lives on even after death in our dreams and in our own eternally shining spirits.

CHAPTER SIX

———

Dreams and Everything Else

———

IS MY LIFE A KIND OF DREAM?

———

Yes, yes, yes! To see this, write down what you saw and felt and did on any given day. Then look carefully at what you have written. You will most likely be able to catch a glimpse of the themes and patterns that are woven throughout your waking hours.

Your life is an amazing web of encounters that have something to teach you. The mewing kitten on the street, the tightly coiled feeling of sadness in your throat, and the unexpected shower of hailstones you experience during the day all have messages to share with you, just as your dream images do.

Whether you are awake or asleep, and whether you can describe it in words or not, the dream that is your life continues to unfold. If you open your senses, you can see something powerful, precious, and alive glistening below the surface of all your experiences—both dreaming and waking. Your wisdom never sleeps!

(To find out more about the waking dream, see Part Three of this book.)

WHY DO I WANT TO SLEEP SO MUCH OF THE TIME?

You may find your eyelids drooping in the middle of the day when you are sick, struggling with some sort of challenge, or when you are emotionally scraping bottom. Wrapping yourself in a cozy blanket of dreams at these times is one way to nurture yourself and see your life from a different perspective. Often, when you awaken from a much-needed nap, you find that the mental knots, the aches and pains of your body, or the nebulous clouds of feeling that were building inside you have been soothed through contact with your own softly flowing inner world.

When big changes are happening to you, you may also need more sleep. During these passages, you are probably doing a tremendous amount of internal work to assimilate the new configurations of your life. Dreams can help you sort through what's happening and find quiet places in which to refresh your spirit.

If you find yourself becoming unusually tired on a regular basis, however, something else may be going on. You may be secretly relying on your dream world as a place of refuge. Even though you may be desperately craving immersion in the beautiful colors of what you see and feel and know while you are awake, you may be telling yourself that there is no time or space for those colors in your waking life. Closing your eyes may be the only way you permit yourself to feel the richness of who you are.

To release your fatigue with the waking world, you might try writing down your answers to some of the following questions:

- What do I need more of in my life?
- What do I really want that I am denying myself?
- What do I need a rest from?
- What do I need to let go of?
- What do I need support with?
- Am I willing to ask either those I know or the universe at large for the support I need?

- What brings me the most joy?
- What can I do to experience my joy more often?

You can also start journaling or writing poetry to express your feelings, or explore your dreams with all the openness you can muster (using exercises like those in Part Two of this book). Or you can set words aside and breathe deeply, walk in the woods, paint, sing, dance, or meditate.

No matter which of these ways you choose to release energy and/or creatively express yourself, remember to listen to your heart. Once you allow yourself to hear what your heart seeks to tell you, your waking life will naturally take on a new shape and tone. Instead of being a solitary island of retreat, your dreams will become one of many channels through which you stay in touch with your spirit. Then your dreams can support you as you express the intricacies of your being here on this warm, brown earth.

CAN DREAMS PREDICT THE FUTURE?

Yes, in a loose sort of way. Though future events are not fixed ahead of time, the decisions we make now can lead us toward certain probable outcomes. And our spirits can send us pictures of those probable outcomes before they come to pass.

Many years ago I decided to receive a psychic reading from a seer who was very good at recognizing what was going on below the surface of her clients' lives. As our meeting drew closer, I became more and more nervous about any surprising information she might share with me. The night before the reading I dreamt that I heard a voice saying, "You can see into the future; anyone can." Then my dreams proceeded to give me a complete outline of what turned out to be the actual reading the seer offered me the next day! I had psychically read my own future psychic reading.

Each of us has this seemingly magical ability to perceive the future, because being able to see into the future is actually a matter of attuning carefully to the present moment. The seeds of the future are being planted right now.

Because our dreaming souls are highly attuned to the reality of what is happening with us at any given time, they can show us the kinds of seeds we are currently planting through our thoughts, words, and actions. They help us to see what events will most likely sprout from the choices we make. In other words, dreams help us to recognize the strongest potential outcome of the paths we're on.

While dreams can foretell events that are likely to come, we need to remember that the future is a changeable, unfolding experience. It is more like a flowing river than a solid rock. If our dreams show us upcoming experiences we don't like, we can shift our attitudes and behaviors and bring forth a brighter future than the one we may have glimpsed in dreams. The sensitivity and creativity that we bring to this moment can always transform the days ahead.

CAN DREAMS PROVIDE HEALING?

Yes. Dreams can put you in touch with the vast part of yourself from which healing springs. This part of you hears what your body, heart, and soul are trying to tell you when you are aching. It understands the base of all your discomfort, and it offers healing advice through dream pictures, stories, and voices.

Sometimes, this advice is very direct. When one of my sons had an ongoing cough, I dreamt that he was standing in a silvery space and a voice told me to give him the herb usnea to dissolve the congestion in his lungs. My conscious mind knew little about this herb so I talked with some herbalists about it. When each of them confirmed my dreams' prescription, I started giving my son this herb and his lungs gradually grew clearer.

This dream remedy was very easy to understand. However, it is not always so. Once when my lower back hurt, I dreamt that a small, happy chipmunk that was precious to me had died the previous year.

At first, I felt confused by this dream, but when I gently immersed myself in what it had to tell me, I found that the chipmunk was the part of my own joy that had died when an important relationship had ended one year before. Because I had not allowed myself to fully experience the grief that loss had caused, it had become dammed up inside me and over-powered my sense of delight.

Exploring this dream helped me to release feelings I had been holding back. Later, when my tears ceased, a profound feeling of calm settled into my heart. At that moment, I knew that new green paths lie ahead for both my former partner and me and that his love would remain with me always. When I stood up, I also found, to my surprise that my back felt relaxed and supple once again! By helping me to release my sadness, my dream had indirectly helped me heal my back.

The healer within you—your soul—speaks with you night after night through your dreams and softly illuminates the fears that limit you. It casts its gentle rays on your sweet, sleeping passions, and helps you to see the true depth and beauty of your own unique being.

If you let them, your dreams will show you again and again that healing can happen in many ways. They will also remind you that the deepest healing comes when you allow yourself to be who you really are in this moment.

CAN DREAMS OPEN DOORS TO GOD, THE GODDESS, BUDDHA, KRISHNA, ALLAH, THE GREAT SPIRIT, AND ALL THAT IS?

I can only answer this question in a very personal manner—for me, they have.

When I was a child, the word "God" brought a colorful and somewhat confusing mix of impressions to my mind. This mix included bits of things I'd learned from my mother's Episcopal church and my father's world of science, as well as realizations I'd had while drawing, writing poetry, and spending time in nature. Often, I didn't know how to reconcile it all. The notions I picked up from important people in my life about the existence or lack of existence of a "greater awareness" didn't always seem to fit with the things that my heart said, or that the stars seemed to whisper to me at night.

However, soon after I became a young adult, I began to experience the Divine in a new way. As I listened to my dreams and allowed my soul to steer me gently through this process, I started to experience a powerful, loving life force flowing through the world. This was not something another human being, organization, or book taught me. It was a kind of knowing that spilled into my pores as I used my dreams to open up to all that lay within me and around me. I began to feel that love was real and that it was huge and that it was everywhere.

During this time, I dreamt about a number of striking spiritual teachers. Once, I saw Jesus walking toward me, enveloping me in a love so enormous that it was overwhelming. Another time, the Dalai Lama appeared and spoke to me about my son. Other nights, I visited with Native American healers and groups of Tibetan lamas. Each of these teachers touched me deeply.

Over time, I have realized that all my dream characters can serve as incredible spiritual teachers for me, whether or not they are acknowledged religious leaders. Each dream character has helped me to see into myself and feel more of the wisdom and kindness that waits there for my recognition. Each one has assisted me in remembering more of what I know about growth, trust, and finding light in dark places. And together, in a collective sense, all my dream characters have had the ability to lead me toward wholeness and a more intimate acquaintance with the Great Spirit that lives within all things.

As I see it, the being so often called by a name like "God" is actually who we are, unfolded one thousand times. We are one with the powerful, loving life force that flows through the world. The more we can let go of fear and step into our real selves, either by exploring our dreams or by traveling down another path of self discovery, the closer we come to God.

God is the essence of who we are deep within.

SUMMARY

Now that you've read Part One, I hope you have a clearer view of your inner wisdom and the manner in which it colors your life and dreams. You also have an idea of some of the ways that wise part of your being, your soul, uses dreams to nudge you toward new growth and healing.

Next, using the exercises in Part Two of this book, you can explore some specific messages within your own dreams. If you don't remember your dreams, or would just prefer to work with your "waking dreams," read over Part Two and then go on and work with the exercises in

Part Three. Remember, you can explore both your sleeping and waking experiences in a conscious, heart-centered way. Enjoy!

PART TWO

Heart-centered Dream Exploration Tools

CHAPTER SEVEN

A Gentle Approach to Dream Exploration

USING THE TOOLS

The tools described in this part of the book can help you recognize the wisdom your soul expresses through your dreams. Each of these tools asks you to feel your dream images rather than analyze them with your intellect. Allow yourself to experiment with these tools. Be adventurous. Find out what happens when you explore a dream without putting your intellect in the driver's seat. Remember that if you practice with these tools over time, they will become easier for you to use. Keep in mind, too, that some of these tools may work better for you than others and that different ones may work better at different moments. Use whichever tools appear the most enticing to you at any given point.

At the end of each tool description, I've included examples of my own dream explorations and the dream explorations of some dear people I know so you can see how the tool works. I hope you find these examples inspiring.

FEELING YOUR FEELINGS
IN DREAM EXPLORATION

As I do the exercises in this book, my attention often waltzes back and forth between my thoughts and my feelings. Sometimes, I can enter into a dream character and feel immediately what she/he/it has to tell me. Other times, if I am already a little distracted, my mind hops around and I try to guess what a certain dream character's message is. When this happens, I become unsure about what that character has to say to me. To refocus my attention on what my dream character feels, I take several deep breaths and imagine myself inside the character. I look out through this character's eyes and feel what she/he/it is feeling.

I know that I am still learning how to listen, really listen, to my feelings, my intuition, and my own inner counsel in a committed way. I am, therefore, compassionate and patient with myself when my rational mind either jumps in to try and figure my dream out or tells me that my explorations don't work. Instead of giving up, I take some deep breaths and love myself with all my fears. I practice listening to my own inner wisdom as fully as I can, and I know that as time goes by, paying attention to what I know deep inside gets easier and easier.

I encourage you to respond to yourself just as gently. Play with these exercises (don't worry about getting them right or wrong), shower yourself with heaps of compassion, and open your heart to yourself one dream character at a time.

ONE NEW INSIGHT AT A TIME

What I try to remember, as I use dream exercises to look below the surface of my dreams, is that I don't need to understand every itsy bitsy image to glean something important from a dream. I do generally probe a dream until it gives me at least one strong, surprising insight. When I receive this insight, I often get a warm, tingly feeling, and I experience a rush of energy (much as I might feel when a massage therapist or an acupuncturist helps me to release a blocked area of energy in my physical body). I begin to feel more at home with my own spirit and more at peace with who I am.

Once this happens I know my dream investigations are "working." I know new channels are opening inside me, and I don't go on to try and comprehend every lovely little nuance of the dream unless I have a burning desire to do that.

If this manner of approaching dream exploration resonates with you, you might want to try making one or two new insights the goal of each of your explorations. Relax the part of your mind that may try to insist on comprehending every little detail of every little dream right now. Instead, give yourself permission to open gently to your own wisdom one step at a time.

ON DAYS WHEN DREAM EXPLORATION IS EXTRA CHALLENGING

If a day comes along when doing these exercises seems more difficult than usual and yet you still would like to do them, try doing the Dialoguing exercise (located in Chapter Nine). Using your heart as the dream character you are working with, ask it what it's feeling, what it fears, what it wants, what it has to teach you, what it needs in order for you to be able to explore your dreams, and what it can tell you about inviting more love into your life.

You can also try using the Inner Wise Woman or Medicine Man Dialogue (located in Part Three) to gain more insights into what's going on with you.

Or you can try taking out a journal and writing down everything you feel about what's going on in your waking life at the moment. What is troubling you? What are you afraid of? What are you yearning for? What would make you happy right now? How would you like to be supported? Once you open to your own feelings more deeply, your dream investigations will become easier.

Exploring our dreams, or any other aspect of our experience, in a conscious, deep-feeling way is no small thing. Our hearts create the bridge between our human experience and our souls; they can lead us to the center of our own true wisdom if we let them. Committing to listening to our own hearts on a regular basis, even when it's not easy, is some of the biggest work we can do in this lifetime.

APPRECIATING DREAMS
WITHOUT SEEKING THEIR MEANING

We can learn a great deal from exploring our dreams, but we also may feel a strong impulse not to do any sort of exploration of images that seem immensely beautiful or touching. These dreams come to us like ripples of light, creating a warm glow in our hearts. We may feel inspired to write them down, or we may want to let go of the need to ask questions or uncover meanings and experience them without words, and that's okay. Sometimes we just need to cherish our dreams and feel them reverberating inside us. We don't want to dilute their impact.

Once I dreamt of running up over the crest of a hill and jumping into the silkiest sand I have ever touched. I can still call up the feeling of that sand, and that's enough for me. I don't want to define the sand, and I don't want to talk it into being more or less than it was. I just want to remember the experience of being enveloped in something so soft.

Listen to yourself. You will know whether or not to explore the meaning of your dream or let your questions dissolve. Embrace your inner knowing.

TRUST YOUR DREAMS

Keep in mind, when you do choose to explore your dreams, that you can trust them. Though dreams may point out areas in which you have more growing to do, they will never tell you anything bad about yourself. Dreams come from the loving center of your being. They help you to see the greater truth of who you are, and they assist you in making choices in your waking life that honor this greater truth.

As you read the following pages and do the exercises, know that you can do this in an atmosphere of loving kindness. Go forth and allow your dreams to gently guide you to a broader understanding of who you are and what your life on earth is all about.

CHAPTER EIGHT

How to Start Exploring Your Dreams

PUTTING YOUR DREAM EXPLORATIONS TOGETHER

Here are some of my favorite ways to do dream exploration:

- If you need help recalling your dreams, be sure to read over Chapter Three.

- When you have a dream or dreams you are ready to explore, choose three dream characters to work with. Practice Point of View (Chapter Nine) with one dream character that interests you, Dialoguing (Chapter Nine) with another, and Dream Body (Chapter

Ten) with another. At another time, choose three characters from one dream and do both Dialoguing and Dream Body. Practice this combination a lot. Dialoguing and Dream Body are probably the two best tools you can use for creating a clear understanding of any given dream. They are the two tools I use the most often, even after more than thirty years of exploring my dreams.

· For a slight variation on the combination I described above, try doing Point of View or Dialoguing with three characters from a dream. Then use Dream Dance (Chapter Ten) for a very enriching and revealing experience. We do this combination regularly in my dream classes, and I highly recommend it.

· If you have a nightmare or an uncomfortable dream, use Dialoguing with one or two characters from the dream, and then do Reworking (Chapter Eleven)

·· On occasion, try the Themes (Chapter Eleven) exercise. If that helps, do the Point of View or Dialoguing exercise with one or two characters from the dream. This exercise also works well at those times when your overall experience in the dream affects you more than the characters and it is not as easy for you to pick out a dream character with which to work.

· Have fun! Play with these exercises in any combination, vary them, or even make up new exercises. Nothing on these pages is set in stone. Everything that's here is meant to inspire you to recognize your own inner wisdom.

CREATING CLOSURE
WITH YOUR EXPLORATIONS

By using one or more of the dream exploration exercises in Part Two, you'll probably stir up some new feelings. If you're concerned that you don't know what to do with all these feelings, and you'd like a greater sense of resolution, try one of the following ideas:

· After you have explored a dream, write down several concise sentences about what you learned from it. Allow yourself to savor your new knowledge or understanding.

· Come up with one new step you could take to enrich your waking life that is based on some insight or insights you gathered from a dream.

- If you feel that your dream explorations have raised important questions rather than providing you with answers, write down your questions and invite your soul to give you feedback about how to resolve these questions. Then, keep your eyes and ears open during the day so that you can spot any feedback from the universe that comes along.

- Imagine the elevated or expanded version of a dream character or theme you've explored. Contemplate this expansion as something you are seeking to experience within yourself and your own life.

- Express your dream, or what you learned from it, in an artistic form. Draw, paint, sculpt, sing, dance, or create a poem, collage, mandala, mobile, or mask.

CHAPTER NINE

─────

First Tools

─────
POINT OF VIEW
─────

The Point of View tool invites you to retell your dream from the point of view of one of your dream characters. Begin by choosing a character from your dreams. A character can be any distinct image in the dream (a person, an object, a plant, or a part of the landscape). For example, you might decide to work with a gnarled old oak tree, a breaching whale, or a giant puddle of yellow goop. The image you pick is up to you, so choose whichever one sparks your curiosity.

Now, take a pen and paper and, if you haven't already done so, write down the part of your dream in which this character appeared. Tell the dream from your own point of view and note the feelings you had while the dream was going on.

Then, write down the dream from the character's point of view. As your character recounts the events, let it tell you about feelings and any insights that were a result of the dream. Maybe the dream character wants to explain actions that were taken in the dream, or tell you what some of the dream characters thought of you.

While doing this exercise, let your character speak freely. Set interpretation aside and immerse yourself in this character, allowing feelings and impressions to tumble out.

Any time your sweet, persistent brain gets in the way and tries to interpret anything that's going on, thank it nicely for its attempt to assist, and ask it to step back out. Return to feeling and listening to this dream character deeply within your heart.

Example One:
From Marsha's Point of View

I dream I am male and I am playing basketball with a team on the basketball court. A woman comes out on the floor. She is an observer and not a player. She puts her arms around me. I feel loved and deeply moved. I ask her what her name is and she says "Elle." I keep repeating the name so I can find her again if we get separated. I feel I have found the other part of myself.

From Elle's Point of View

I come to the game and immediately spot a person on the basketball court who is in need of female touch and nurturing, someone hungry for love. I know I am interrupting the game, but I go ahead and rise out on the floor to offer Marsha a hug and human touch. What I want her to know is that she has been working too hard, even in her play. I would ask her to slow down, to "be" rather than to "do." Marsha has been pushing herself too hard and has become competitive in a way that does not serve her. I would encourage her to focus on nurturing herself, connecting with others in the heart, and tuning into the essence of love that surrounds us all always. I would also like to remind her to allow intuition to rule and to follow those inner urges that can lead to true magic and meaning. Most importantly I'd like to tell her to love, love, love herself and to remember that she and I are one.

Example Two:
From Jude's Point of View

My young son is holding up a toilet seat and repeatedly touching it on the inside. I feel a little disgusted by what he's doing, and I tell him that it is not okay. He doesn't agree with me and does it anyway. I try to scare him out of doing it by talking to him about the threat of unpleasant illnesses like hepatitis A.

From Toilet Seat's Point of View

I am a symbol of "letting go." I am here to talk with you about the way you mentally push aside people, events, and ideas that you no longer need in your life. Jude, your son is here because he is curious about what happens when he releases something from his life. He wants to see everything with clear eyes and to know everything with a clear mind. You, on the other hand, sometimes neglect to bring this kind of attention to the experience of outgrowing something. A great deal of love moves through you, but you occasionally step out of its flow and become afraid that the past will tie you down and keep you from moving forward if you don't ignore it, or look down your nose at it. You don't trust the strength of the growth force within you. Sometimes, you forget to appreciate the fact that the past, with all its detours and mistakes, helped to lay the foundation upon which you stand now.

Your son does not accept this kind of attitude from you. Because of who he is and also because of his great love for you, he challenges you to embrace all your experiences—even the parts that you don't think are nice. Remember that releasing the old is an important part of the creation of the new. Do not blindly reject your previous choices, even if they start to seem silly, cumbersome, or shortsighted. Learn from your son and respect the whole cycle of life and death—the way that pooping (letting go) is a part of being. New inspirations and opportunities will arise seamlessly when you release the past in a kind and thoughtful way. Open your heart and lay the past to rest with love.

Example Three:
From Kate's Point of View

I am on my way to visit Sarah, a little girl who (in waking life) lived nearby when my daughter was growing up. In the dream, Sarah, about ten, has been moving from here to there and living in parent-amplified squalor. Her present home environment consists of mountains of junk crammed into shacks on a rundown property, some of which might later be crammed onto her family's truck and moved with them. Poor little girl! I feel sadness, a yearning to help her, and a sense of near-hopelessness and frustration at the chaos and selfishness of the family. Sarah needs friends and a solid life, but her parents stand in the way. How can I help her? Whatever I give Sarah, the parents always take from her for their own use. Oh God—shades of my own childhood and that of the real Sarah, plus the very thing that's in the way of my human connections now: chaos, memories of pathetic parents, and confusion about what was/is currently needed.

I want to give Sarah a birthday present, something useful. A distant relative has sent her a rather beat-up handful of tiny pink rosebuds, and my husband, Andre, has given her a rose stem that is dried up but that will bloom when put in water (the same tiny pink roses, fully open). I feel touched by these gifts and by other people who are trying to let Sarah know she is pretty, lovable, and worthy. I ask Sarah what she wants as a birthday present, and she struggles to find an answer. Finally, she says, "Tinkerbell stationery." Does she want this so she can keep in touch with friends from all the places she's briefly stayed? I realize, for her present to be useful, I'll also need to give her stamps and an address book. I worry that her dad might take the stamps if he knows about them.

After giving Sarah these things, I tell her parents that I hope they'll come and camp at my house. I have mixed feelings about saying this, because I want to take care of Sarah and help her somehow, but I know it would be dangerous to get connected with her family in any way (as it would be in waking life).

In the last part of the dream, I am on some sort of trip and trying to figure out how to get back home from a remote mountain area. I'm going to try and buy a bicycle in a little town that reminds me of Laramie, the place I lived in waking life until authorities removed me from my family of origin at age thirteen.

From Sarah's Point of View

I am living with my parents in some shacks near a high mountain town. Today was my birthday. One of my relatives sent me a bouquet of tiny roses and they weren't in very good shape when they got here. I was glad my relatives remembered me, though. Someday, I'll get roses that are all still pretty and pink. Also, Kate came to see me—all the way from the coast! I was glad to see her. Sometimes, I miss her and the art projects we did with all the neighborhood kids, but I try not to think about that, because doing it makes my life now seem worse. Anyway, she brought me a dried-up stem of a rose from Andre and said that if I put it in water, it would blossom. Hearing that made me want to cry. Did Andre like me? I hardly knew him! Then she asked me what I wanted for my birthday. Funny, I've been waiting for someone to ask me that question, but at the same time I've been afraid of it. It's like wanting anything just sets me up for more disappointment; it's safer not to want anything. Good things don't come to people in my family, and anything I want seems so selfish and useless. So I had a hard time even knowing what I want, let alone telling her. At last I thought of Tinkerbell stationery, because one of my friends once had it. I wanted to be like that girl—to have her parents, her house, her clothes, her things, her friends, and her life. I wanted everything clean and pretty and feminine, and lots of friends to write notes to.

I could never tell my parents I wanted something like Tinkerbell stationery, but I thought Kate might understand. She's sort of into magic and pretty things. Thinking about that stationery made me happy. It was something so different, so special, and it kind of made me feel like I could talk to my old friends—even though I don't know how to reach them. I wonder if I could get some of my friends' addresses; maybe one of my old teachers could help me. Maybe Kate could help me.

I was kind of embarrassed when Kate saw our house. She and I needed something from the kitchen and then she saw what the kitchen was like—how hard it was even to get a glass of water! Oh well. Later, she invited us all to her house to camp if we ever got back to the coast again. She must still like me. I wish I could tell her how I feel! I wish I could go and live with her! I wish I could stay in one place and have a real house and real friends! Oh, but wishes can break your heart over and over! I keep a certain distance from people for that reason. I know we'll never go camp at her house, not really. It's just as well, because maybe my dad would burn her house down or get in a fight or get arrested. And maybe my mom would steal something from Kate and Andre, or try to get them to give her stuff. I don't know. Then Kate would never speak to me again; she would be afraid or mad or something.

I hate this life! I hate it! I wish I were grown up and on my own! I can't wait to be on my own. Then no one can mess everything up!

P.S. Kate got me the Tinkerbell stationery, but then she left. I can't bring myself to look at it yet, because I'm afraid I will cry. I'm scared to show it to my parents, because they might not want me to have it. I put the rose stem from Andre in water and now it's blooming; I can look at that without crying, but it does make me sort of happy/sad.

I wish I could tell Kate that I love her and that she made a difference in my life. I would tell her to keep doing art with kids 'cuz doing that makes her happy. When Kate is happy, she's kind and patient and generous and really, really smart.

I would ask her what she wanted for her birthday, and I wouldn't leave till she told me and I got it for her. I hope it would be something as magical as Tinkerbell stationery.

DIALOGUING

This tool is the one I've used the most to expand my understanding of dreams. It allows me to explore a dream character in depth and talk intimately with part of my own spirit. If you do this exercise with a character that appeared in a scary or uncomfortable context, I highly recommend that you do the Reworking exercise (Chapter Ten) after you have completed this one. I also encourage you to try the last question in the set listed on page 90. It has to do with seeing a character in its most expanded, radiant, and elevated form.

To begin, get a pen and some paper. Then choose a dream character to explore. If you haven't done so already, write down a description of the dream in which this character appears.

Next, come up with some questions you'd like to ask this character, or pick some of the following:

- How do you feel?
- What do you have to teach me? (Sometimes, if this question doesn't feel as though it has an easy answer,

I ask instead: What is it that you know a lot about, or that you know how to do particularly well, that you would like to share with me?)

- What part of me are you?
- What can you teach me about inviting more love into my life?
- What would you be like in your most expanded, radiant, and elevated form? (This is a powerful question, and one I highly recommend asking. I have only recently been using it, so you won't see it included in the examples given in this chapter.)

The questions listed above are probably the key ones you'll want to work with. However, if you ask those questions and still don't have a feeling of resolution, see if you can turn your sense of uncertainty, concern, or fear into one or more questions for your character.

For instance, a woman I know recently did a dialogue with her own heart. Her heart told her that it wanted her to "follow her heart." She accepted this idea intellectually but was still afraid of making a "wrong decision" in her life that could hurt others' feelings. I suggested that she ask her heart what it could tell her about making a wrong decision in life. Asking this question helped her to address one of her own fears and understand her heart's message in a more concrete way.

You can also try any of the following questions that you feel drawn to:

- What are you doing in this dream and why are you doing it?
- How do you see me?
- What do you need most from me?

- How are you appearing in my waking life right now?

If the character is one that scares you or that seems to be doing something destructive, you can ask:

- What is it you are trying to protect, or express, or release?
- Is there a way I could help you that will not seem threatening or destructive to me?
- Is there some beautiful aspect of myself I am forgetting to trust and admire?

When you are ready to start the dialogue, relax, breathe deeply, and write down your first question. Imagine that you are asking your dream character this question. Then "step inside" of your character. Allow yourself to feel how this character would like to answer. Be the character as they answer the question. What would you say as this character? Write down whatever you hear, whatever responses come rising up from within you, and be sure to use the word "I." The idea here is not to talk about the character, but rather to be the character, to feel its responses from the inside out.

If one question does not bring a clear answer, ask a different question, or ask the same question in a different way. Be patient and remain open to any perceptions this character has to share with you.

Note that this tool works best when you stay present with feelings. Give yourself permission to embody what this character is feeling and what they have to tell you. If you get an urge to start interpreting what's going on, gently guide yourself back into the realm of the heart once again. Remind yourself that you are focusing on what this character feels.

You may ask as many questions as you need to in order to understand this character's message. When you are done, thank this part of yourself for offering you its wisdom.

Example One:
Claire's Dream

I was part of a group of people sitting in lawn chairs across from another group of people. I went over to check on the other people just to make sure they were all alive and happy. They were, but they were sitting in a line of garden plots and one of the plots was dead. Everyone was avoiding it. We were due to launch somewhere and this plot was holding us up. There was also another plot owned by an elderly man that was filled with some dead or dying flowers and a "crazy woman" sitting in a lawn chair. She was ungrounded, wearing lots of jewelry, clothes in a variety of pink colors, and makeup. She did not want to garden. Besides this plot and the dead one, the place was beautiful.

Dialogue with the Dead Yard

Claire: How do you feel?

Dead yard: I am barely breathing. I'm still, dry, joyless, and ignored.

Claire: Who are you?

Dead yard: I am a part of you that you don't want to acknowledge; I'm not interested in living.

Claire: Even if you were in a relationship again, loving and giving?

Dead yard: That's not going to take care of the problem. I don't care about life, and that's why the plants are dead.

Claire: What's going on that you don't care about life?

Dead yard: The minerals are gone and the soil is yucky, not fertile. Deep down is okay, but nobody can get to it.

Claire: What would need to happen in order for the soil to be mineral rich, yummy, and fertile?

Dead yard: Claire would be gardening and getting her hands in the earth, paying attention to the plants; she'd be living from deeper inside.

Claire: Do you mean that needs to be her focus right now, rather than doing healing work with people?

Dead yard: She'd be much happier.

Claire: It looks like you're coming back to life as we talk. Wildflowers and grasses are coming up. Is there anything else you'd like to say to Claire?

Dead yard: Yes. Let yourself develop your love for gardening.

Dialogue with the Crazy Woman

Claire: What's the most important thing to you?

Crazy woman: Maintaining a pretty face and looking good— in pink and with jewelry. I will get dirty if I garden!

Claire: So you really don't like to get dirty and wear funky gardening clothes?

Crazy woman: Oh no! I've got to control things and maintain how I look. At least this I can somewhat control. Gardening—working with nature and bugs—is so uncontrollable and frustrating.

Claire: What would it take for you to garden a bit and come down to earth?

Crazy woman: I'd like to wear pink, a big hat, sunscreen, nice things, maybe even a necklace, a pink stone necklace! Earrings are a given. I want to be a woman not a boy. I can feel so boyish when gardening—androgynous—I don't like that!

Claire: Wow! Well, that all sounds like something I can do for you—the pink-loving, feminine part of myself—so that I/you can feel comfortable gardening.

Crazy woman: Good. I also need you to nurture me with lots of water and electrolyte drinks. And I want you to give me breaks. Too much work is not feminine; it hurts. You really need to listen to me. Otherwise, you go out of your body and feel loopy. If you can listen to me, then we can do the gardening that will make you happy.

Example Two:
Forest's Dream

Note: My son Forest was nine years old when we did this exercise out loud together. Notice how succinct these exercises can become when you do them with a child.

In this TV show, some guys were trying to kill a certain spirit. They thought they had done it. But I saw this huge face up on the ceiling above them. I knew the spirit was not dead.

Dialogue with the Spirit

Ana Lora: How are you feeling?

Spirit (voiced by Forest): I want to be powerful.

Ana Lora: What do you have to teach Forest?

Spirit: What he's seeing is not always what he thinks he's seeing.

Ana Lora: What do you mean?

Spirit: He needs to look for love in all situations. Sometimes, he only notices what is unloving.

Ana Lora: Do you feel complete?

Spirit: Yes.

Example Three:
Forest's Dream

Note: This was another one I did with Forest when he was nine years old.

I was in a building. I heard heavy breathing. Someone was behind me, following me. I was afraid. Later on, after I'd left this building, I was in a place where there were a couple of doors I could go through. Papa and someone else went through another door. The door I went in took me back inside the building to the place where I was afraid.

Dialogue with the Guy
Who was Following Forest

Ana Lora: How are you feeling?

Guy who was following Forest (voiced by Forest): I want to be alone.

Ana Lora: How do you feel about Forest?

Guy: I want him to leave.

Ana Lora: Is there something you have to teach Forest?

Guy: He needs not to just do things the way other people do them. He needs to find his own way to do things.

Ana Lora: Has he been forgetting this?

Guy: Yes.

Ana Lora: Do you feel complete?

Guy: Yes.

Ana Lora: Thank you.

Example Four:
Ana Lora's Dream

Note: When I had this dream, I was working as a certified massage therapist in waking life and struggling to find my identity as a healer. I wondered if the kind of healing I really wanted to do was best described as massage therapy, hands-on-healing, or something else. .

In one corner of a room inside a public library, a man wants me to massage him. As I begin to do this, he immediately gets mad at me for not digging deeply enough into the muscles in his shoulder area.

Dialogue with the Man
Who Wants Me to Dig

Ana Lora: Who are you?

Man: I am your self-criticism, your anger at yourself for not being able to be a hundred million things to a hundred million people. You are missing your own particular grace, your own primary gifts, by wanting to be "all." When you call yourself a massage therapist, in your mind, you broaden the spectrum too much of what you are willing to do or try and do for others. You become ensnared by self-expectations. Perhaps you need to come up with another title that more accurately describes what you share with individuals in your "hands-on healing" work.

Ana Lora: What do you have to teach me?

Man: You are not meant to be digging into my shoulder with all your might. That is not your work. Leave that to someone who has bigger thumbs or pointier elbows and who is not as sensitive as you are. You were given the gift of sensitivity so that you could use it, rather than sheer physical strength, in your work.

Release your own anger at yourself for not being as physically strong as this man demands you to be and for sensing this limitation in your being. All human beings, even healers, have limitations and unique strengths, roads they choose not to travel and roads they leap onto wholeheartedly. Choose the road that uses your strengths and that brings you the most joy.

Ana Lora: Do you have anything else to share with me?

Man: Your work is to touch people with your presence and your vision. When you write your warm words, draw your soft pictures, or place your gentle hands on someone's body during a healing session, you help them to know that they are seen and held in a great, tender love—a love that extends far beyond you. That is what you do well and that is the work you are meant to be doing.

Ana Lora: Thank you.

Man: You are most welcome.

CHAPTER TEN

Dreaming Down to Your Toes

DREAM BODY

Your body has an intuition of its own. Deep in your bones, your muscles, and each of your cells is a kind of knowing that often differs from the knowledge you can detect through your mind. With the following exercise you can use your body's awareness to explore the messages your soul sends you through dreams.

To begin, choose a dream character to explore. (Characters are described at the beginning of the Point of View exercise in the previous chapter.)

Now move your body into a position that feels the way this character *feels* to you (not the way the character looks). As you do this, you might want to consider the following questions:

- Does this character seem as though it needs to be low to the ground or up high?
- Is this character's energy heavy or light? hard or soft? big or small? active or passive? old or new? consistent or wobbly? strong or weak? contracted or open? confused or clear?

Now notice what this position feels like. How does your body respond to this pose? Is it one that's familiar to your body in any way?

Feel the energy of this character in your feet . . . your calves . . . your knees . . . your thighs . . . your pelvis . . . your stomach . . . your chest . . . your bottom . . . your back . . . your arms . . . your hands . . . your shoulders . . . your neck . . . your face . . . and your whole head.

Feel it from the top of your head to your toes. Feel it up and down your spine. Let yourself be filled with this character's energy.

Now imagine that you are this character. Begin to explore some movements that reflect your unique way of being. If you like, you can add words or sounds that you feel tell something about who you are.

When you feel you have absorbed all the information you can receive this way, breathe deeply, release this character's energy from your body, and bring it into your heart. Then come back to your whole self.

If you would like to learn more about this character, try the Dialoguing exercise in Chapter Nine, or the Dream Dance exercise, with this character and two others.

DREAM DANCE

This exercise is an expansion of the Dream Body exercise. You will explore three different dream characters that reflect several parts of who you are and let them move together in one evolving dance.

To begin, choose three different dream characters, preferably from the same dream.

Do the Dream Body exercise with each one.

Now step into the body position you chose to represent your first dream character. Feel this position fully.

Then gradually shift into the body position you chose for the second character. Notice what changes take place as you shift from the first character into the second.

Now start moving slowly into the body position for the third character. Pay attention to the changes that occur as you move from the second dream character into the third.

After you have come fully into the body position for the third character, gradually begin moving back into the body position for the first character. Again, feel any changes as you do this.

Pass through this whole sequence, moving slowly from one character into the next, several times.

Now you are going to move through all three characters again, but this time "elevate" or expand any of the characters that don't feel completely good to you or that feel somewhat weak, dark, or contracted. How can you shift them so that they feel bigger, stronger, clearer, wiser, or brighter? How could they be more open, more loving, or more grounded in their own unique gifts?

Move slowly from one character to the next, experiencing each of these three characters in their fullest potential. Do this several times.

Then let the whole thing become a dance. Allow these different aspects of who you are to mix and samba with each other. Feel the strengths of each of them. Feel how they can support one another. Let each of these aspects of yourself move together in greater harmony.

Finally, allow these diverse parts of who you are blend together and move as one. Open yourself up to embrace all of them at once. Dance with this new sense of wholeness for as long as you like.

When you feel that this dance is done, find a way to end it. Close your eyes and settle into stillness. Breathe deeply and release these characters from your body. Then, focus and contemplate all that you felt.

When you feel ready, open your eyes and make any notes that you wish to about what you experienced/felt.

CHAPTER ELEVEN

*More Tools
for Understanding*

THEMES

If you look carefully at your dreams, you can see themes there that reflect lessons you are seeking to learn in your waking life. By doing this exercise you can explore what some of these themes mean to you.

To begin, write down one complete dream. Record both the images in the dreams and the feelings these images bring up.

Notice any connecting threads in what you have written. You can probably do this intuitively, but if you need a little help, try looking for similar images or emotions in different parts of the dream and any strongly contrasting ones. (Steer away from this method, however, if it puts you too much "in your head.")

If your dream is a short one that doesn't have a lot of images, just note your overall impression of the dream—its most powerful aspect.

After this, give the dream a title that identifies the main theme or themes in the dream.

Now free associate on this theme. Write about how you sense it weaving its way through your life, asking you to expand in certain directions. Can you feel what this theme means to you? What does this theme tell you about something you know deep inside? How does exploring this theme give you some new insights into your waking life? How does it help you to awaken some part of your heart?

Let the words come out in a free-flowing stream, without filtering or analysis. You don't even need to write in whole sentences. Just allow your feelings to pour out. If you like, you can also draw pictures of this theme or make a collage about it, using magazine images and found objects.

Example One: Rebecca's Dream

I am hiking up a trail to a lake in the Trinity Alps. The trail is easier than the one I usually take when I am backpacking up to this lake in waking life. I stop overnight at a place along the trail that is crowded with people and tents. There are even bathroom stalls here. The whole area is very popular and trampled. It is dry, dusty, and lacking the pristine beauty I know I can find on the other, harder trail I have traveled on before. That trail has waterfalls next to it and breathtaking scenery all around. I am not sure whether I want to stay on this new, easier, overused trail or go back to the other more natural one.

In the second part of this dream, I am with a group of people who are partnering with one another to sing a song about mountains and other places of earthly magnificence. Somehow, singing the song helps to protect and preserve those areas. I can feel this song inside myself: I know how to sing it even without the written music before me, and that feels good.

One man in our group says to another that he doesn't want to partner with him. He wants to wait for a teacher who "really knows" the words to the song before he sings. Yet no teacher like this comes and the two men do end up partnering.

Quest for Beauty Dream

I am missing the beauty here by following the broad, dusty path. This is the way that many feet pass. Is this the path I'm meant to be on? I like the ease of this route. I enjoy the feeling of hard, flat, beaten-down dirt under my hiking shoes. It's a nice change from the "steep slopes" I so often find myself climbing up in my life.

I want my life to be easier. I want to tromp along an enormously wide trail with very little incline. And I want to be able to see the bright colors of others' shirts as they travel ahead of me on the path, showing me exactly where to go. This is what I want. Or is it?

The greatest beauty lies on the other, narrower path that curves more steeply uphill—the one that challenges my breath, my muscles, every fiber of my being. There are no hordes of people on that greener trail, charting out my steps. It is a wilder place. And yet, a distinct trail is visible to me there.

I guess, ultimately, I seek the less traveled route. I am willing to trip over rocks, to deal with obstacles if I have to, to plod slowly along to new heights if that is the way I need to go to touch the exquisite core of all existence. I do choose beauty over convenience, though, I would like to allow more of a sense of ease in my life, too.

For years I have felt called to lead meditation groups and offer healing sessions to others. I've believed that these were good ways both to call forth my own joy and to serve the world. Yet, my path hasn't always been easy. There has never been a well-trampled trail before me to show me exactly where to go. Sometimes, I have stepped forward with confidence, giving what is mine to give. Other times, my fears and lack of self-esteem have caused me to backpedal. I have been like the man who waits for an accomplished teacher to come before he will partner up and offer his love and support to the earth through song. He waits to encounter a person greater than himself before he will participate, and no one any more adept than himself ever appears. He doubts himself, and so do I.

Looking at this dream, I wonder if there is some part of me that holds back from giving what is mine to give, that thinks my voice and "the song I have to sing" is not good enough to share? Can I encourage myself to be expressive anyway, even though my attempts are a little awkward sometimes? Can I let go of my desire for perfection and focus, instead, on calling forth all the loveliness and grace that is mine to know?

This dream affirms that I do know the song that is mine to sing. Upon further reflection, I realize that I want to join with others to release into the world all the music that lives deep in our hearts. I want to surrender any residual fears of imperfection so that I can give what I have to give without reservations. I want to step strongly onto my own path of beauty, even if it is a bit steep and rocky at times, and go wherever it asks me to go.

Example Two:
Jim's Dream

Someone who felt extremely angry toward me entered my house and threatened me. I'm not sure which house from my past it was, or if it was a house the dream made up. It could have been 100 Lake Forest, my home from age five to twenty-six. I felt very frightened at first, but instead of remaining fearful, I became angry with the invader and tearful at the same time. I began to scream at him, because this person had killed my mother and father. At the same time, I knew that he hadn't really killed them but had attacked my positive image of them. In any event, he weakened and began to withdraw. What began as a possible nightmare was transformed before it became one.

True Self Versus Ego

In this dream, I am standing up to a wounded, angry part of myself (the intruder). My emerging sense of self is challenging the old aspect of my being that has blamed my parents and my history for all my fears and anxieties. In other words, the timeless portion of who I am, is coming forward and prevailing over the part of me that has allowed the pain I experienced in the past and my fears about the future to eclipse my experience of the current moment. I feel this dream comes up because, in my waking life, I want to remain present without fear in a relationship that is slowly growing intimate.

Over the years, I have had many dreams containing this theme of "home invasion by fearful forces." In all of these dreams, I have usually awakened myself in order to end the nightmare. This dream, however, was distinctly different. This was the first time I struck back at the invading alien energy. I regard it as a dream of transformation. Looking at this dream has helped me step further outside an old pattern of setting my parents up as scapegoats for the fearful way I have conducted myself in all of my intimate relationships. In the past, I've persuaded myself that blaming them was justified, since their actions were the catalysts for many of my fears, but I need to stop the cycle of getting stuck in my fears and then blaming them. My emergence from this cycle of fear and blame began quite some time ago, but this long struggle may now be over in a more complete sense.

In the new intimate relationship I have entered in my waking life (the outcome of which is quite uncertain), I initially experienced a return to serious anxiety, depression, and a tendency to sweep feelings under the rug, but I did not remain there. Instead, I began to communicate from a position of strength, clarity, and love that is from my "being" rather than my ego. It took doing this a few times to arrive at a place of comfort and confidence, but then I was able to speak from my true self more easily rather than communicating from a perspective of "old pain."

This may be the most important dream I've had. It reminds me that I am approaching my new relationship and its uncertain future with only isolated moments of fear. It also helps me to know that when moments of fear do arrive, I can move through them.

Example Three:
Ana Lora's Dream

On this night, I dream of David. In waking life David was a brilliant childhood friend of my brother's whom I'd lost contact with after we'd both grown up. All I knew about his adult life was that he had realized he was gay after which he moved to NYC and then written a book about his experiences. The book mainly detailed a long string of casual sexual relationships he'd had with other men. When my brother sent the book to me to read, I felt saddened by the feelings of emptiness and unresolved longing I found in its pages. Several years after the book was published, David died of AIDS.

In this dream, I am ecstatic to discover a new book that reveals the real David. The new book doesn't describe his astonishing intellect or unrealized quest for fulfillment. Instead, it emphasizes the incredible richness in the center of his being, and I am delighted to share this new perspective with my brother.

In the next part of the dream, I am standing on the street where I grew up, next to the house where my childhood friend Laurie lived. In waking life, Laurie was a girl whom the rest of us neighborhood kids considered selfish and bossy.

In this dream I am overjoyed to discover that Laurie has grown into a receptive and kind woman, one who is open in all directions, and who has written a book that reflects all this. I can see the grace within her when I look at her . . . and I am moved beyond words.

While I am gazing at Laurie, suddenly her dog steps out. (In waking life Laurie owned a fierce German shepherd who attacked me when I was eight years old.) In this dream, Laurie's dog is a HUGE Doberman pinscher with an aggressive demeanor. When I see him, I think, "Uh oh." My son Canyon is standing a little ways away from me by a row of trees and he has caught the dog's attention. I feel a wave of rising panic as I realize I am too far away to protect my son. All I can do is call to Canyon and tell him to get close to one of the trees and stand still. Upon hearing my voice, however, the dog turns his attention and begins coming after me. I feel intensely afraid.

Yet, just when I think my rapidly beating heart will explode with terror, what I am seeing before me breaks up, like a scrambled TV image. In that instant, I believe both the dog and I simultaneously shift out of our old patterns. As he comes closer, he stops projecting aggression and gently peers at me out of large sweet eyes . . . and I release my fear and go down on both knees to greet him. While I pet him, he nuzzles me, just as if I were the cutest human he'd ever discovered.

Finding the Whole Truth Dream

There have been times in my life when I have allowed myself to experience only a tiny, hard-shelled version of my real self. At those moments, I did not realize how small my range of vision had become, how tough my shell was, or how much I had cut myself off from the amazing life and love that always seeks to flow through me.

Like my brother's friend, David, I've used my wounded intellect to search for happiness not realizing that I could live from the center of my own beautiful soul and find fulfillment there. Like my old friend Laurie, I have, sometimes, become tightly focused on my own personal agenda, which eclipsed my natural ability to experience a deep sense of communion with myself and others. (I have told myself that I have to make this or that project happen by myself . . . that I don't have time to slow down, listen fully, or breathe in the subtler fragrances in this world because I have something I have to get DONE.) And like the big, fierce dog, I have had moments in which I became overprotective of myself or something that I treasured, not recognizing that if I could allow myself to feel the power of my own open-hearted gentleness, I wouldn't need to do any fierce posturing with the world around me.

Recently, I've been seeking to release fear on many levels in my waking life. Whenever I feel fear coming to the surface, I tell myself, "that's an old fear that I don't need to be limited by any more." Then I set my intention clearly and remind myself of what I do want in my life—love, connection, joy, ease, and the ability to offer and receive support. I also remind myself over and over throughout the day that I am a channel of love. I tell myself that love flows into my life from all directions and it flows out of me in all directions.

My dream illustrates the effect that these kinds of thoughts and actions can have. It helps me to see that parts of myself that have been wounded, contracted, or heavily defended (as represented by David, Laurie, and the Doberman pinscher) are actually beginning to heal in significant ways. In a way I can't explain, it helps me feel the power of opening my heart to my own inner beauty.

REWORKING

We usually have uncomfortable dreams or nightmares when we are keeping a tenacious grip on some mental picture or belief about reality that is not serving us. To release these kinds of dreams and open up our thinking, I recommend doing one of two things.

First, use the Dialoguing exercise and talk to one of the central characters in your unpleasant dream. See if you can get to the bottom of what's going on. What is this character trying to tell you? What part of you is stuck? What beautiful aspect of yourself are you forgetting to trust and admire? How could you enlarge your vision of yourself and the world right now? How could you allow more love and creativity into your life? If you can look deeply at where you are stuck and bring your heart's wisdom there, I guarantee you will get unstuck.

Another thing you can do in combination with Dialoguing, or just by itself, is to modify the image in your mind that is creating the unpleasantness in your dreams and in your life. When you change the picture, you effectively change your mind. Your dreams do a magnificent job of showing you the mental picture that is causing you problems. With the following exercise you get to change that picture.

You will be writing down one scene from a dream two times. The first time, write down a scene that bothers you. Alternatively, you can draw an actual picture of it. When you write or draw the scene the second time, transform it into one you feel good about. What would you like to see happen in this scene? How can you change the scene into an experience that delights you? Bring all your true power, grace, and humor into play as you do this. Rework this image in one or more ways until it begins to feel good.

After you have done this, in the days that follow, keep bringing this reworked dream image to mind and see what effect changing this dream has on you and your life.

This is a great exercise to do with kids who have had nightmares. Ask the child who has had a nightmare to change the dream, to make it into something they feel happy about, and then draw a picture of this "new dream."

Example One:
Canyon's Dream

Note: My son Canyon had this dream when he was ten.

I crashed down some buildings by mistake. I broke a lot of glass and an angry policeman was coming to get me.

Reworking Options: I asked Canyon to change the dream into one he'd feel better about, but he wasn't sure how to do that. I suggested that maybe the policeman could realize that he hadn't meant to destroy the buildings and instead of being angry at Canyon, the policeman could help him build some new buildings. Or maybe the policeman could come running up and swing Canyon around in a jolly dance right before he ran into the buildings. My younger son Forest was eight at the time, and he had been listening to all this. Forest said, "Or maybe the policeman realizes that those buildings need to be crashed down and he comes and jumps on them with you!" (That last option was Canyon's favorite.)

Example Two:
Tim's Dream

Note: In Tim's contribution to this section, he provides some background information so that you can understand the context in which this dream appeared in his life. You do not have to write down any background information when you are doing this exercise yourself, unless you want to.

I am going down this enormous hill on a wide, open road in a small truck or jeep that has no steering wheel. I feel as if I am plummeting down at a fast rate of speed. While this is happening, I can hear several women talking off to the side of the road.

As I drive and my fear increases, I shift around in a way that causes the seat I have been holding onto—the one in front of me—to come entirely out of its socket. Now I have nothing to hold onto.

Somehow I steer my vehicle toward the side of the road where the women are standing and call out to them for help. One of the women sees me and understands what's going on. She grabs my vehicle as I come close and stops me. I thank her.

Background: Among the underlying beliefs I have held for a long time is one that goes something like this: My life is hard. My dreams can come true, but I have to work like crazy and struggle like mad if I want this to happen . . . and even then things don't always work out. (Doesn't sound too fun, does it?)

Anyway, over the years, I have had many dreams that have illustrated my belief that my life needs to be dauntingly difficult. Often, I have pictured myself driving up hills so steep I become afraid that the car I am in will slide down out of control, or fall over backward.

Yet, recently, as I have come to experiment with the idea that my life can be more fun and easy, I have had dreams of going downhill, on wide, open roads, with no obstacles before me. Initially, these dreams thrilled me. But one of the last ones—the one I described above—scared me.

I came up with two ways of reworking this dream that helped me to feel better about gathering momentum and surrendering to the downhill experience.

Reworking Option 1: I make sure that the steering mechanism works in my car before I take off. At the same time I make an inner commitment to "go with the flow" of the experience and not try to control things too much or grip the steering wheel too tightly. As I descend the big hill, the buildup of momentum does scare me, but the women who were on the roadside (in my original dream) are in the car with me this time to provide support. They are ready to encourage and advise me and they have extra sets of controls so they can help me if I panic. This allows me to feel secure enough to start cruisin'!

Reworking Option 2: As in the option above, I prepare for my downhill experience by making sure that the steering mechanism works and by committing myself to the ease of the ride as fully as I can. When I head downward on the wide, open road the buildup of momentum does scare me a little, so I take breaks at pit stops along the side of the road. The volunteers who have stationed themselves there offer me sustenance, friendly conversation, luxurious neck and shoulder massages, and any other pampering I might need. This helps me to feel more relaxed and confident when I roll on down the hill.

Example Three:
Kate's Dream

I dreamt that Andre (my husband) and I had sold our house and we were looking for something new, something smaller, because we couldn't afford as much. We were in a place like the Bay Area, looking for two rooms somewhere. Andre didn't like anything, because he thought the places all seemed so ordinary and lower middle class. I felt frustrated because it seemed to me that we were losing our house in the first place because of him, and now his values (snobbish, indecisive, fearful) were keeping us from getting another place. I thought he was getting us screwed.

Then, on the same trip, when we were in a shop, he realized that he'd lost one of his bags while we'd been shopping. So I began looking around the shop for the missing bag, and I asked him to help me. He whined that there wasn't any point and that one would never be found; he went on and on. The woman shopkeeper said quietly to me that she wanted to clobber him for the way he was behaving. It suddenly lost my temper and crumpled a lamp shade with my hand. I wrecked some other small thing, but don't remember what it was. Then I told Andre he'd have to pay for it. It was hard to contain my rage. I felt so stuck with this idiot.

The dream wound on and on, but my memory fades out. There was something about eating out and spilling food, and getting angry again, but I can't recall it.

Reworking: Andre and I have sold our house and we're looking for something we can afford in the Bay Area. We have a disagreement about what is important. He seems really fussy to me and I'm discouraged by the whole thing. I'm starting to blame him for selling our house and for his combination of indecisive fearfulness and exaggerated expectations, when I realize that I can sit down with him and make a plan.

So we go to a restaurant for lunch, and while we're eating we make a list of all our reasons for selling our old house and buying one in the Bay Area. We list that both of us want a more creative, colorful, and connected life with less to take care of physically. And we want to return to our city "roots." About what we want to buy, I tell him that his dissatisfaction with everything is making it really hard for me.

I need to know what is important to both of us and to make a decision based on that.

Andre says that someplace clean, simple, and easy to take care of is topmost for him. And he doesn't want a "depressing" neighborhood or scary neighbors. For me, I want a colorful neighborhood with really good public transportation that is not too far from lots of interesting things that go on. I'd like a cheerful, fun-to-fix sort of place that has reasonable space for cooking and writing. As soon as we each start to envision this place, as it becomes real in our minds, we resume driving around and looking.

Then, almost like magic, the first place we find after our planning session is perfect and affordable; it's a tiny place in Sausalito (there's a miraculous inheritance hidden somewhere in this dream), on the slope right by the ferry! We are amazed that we can afford a place in such a location. It is small, for sale by owner, and in need of repair, but otherwise wonderful and charming, in a Mediterranean sort of way. We can't wait to get to know the neighbors!

As we unpack in the new house, Andre discovers that the shopping bag full of things he just picked up in San Francisco is missing. He becomes more and more worked up about it. I can feel my skin growing warmer. Then suddenly, he stops, looks straight at me in a knowing way, and we both begin laughing. It is as if we'd both realized at the same moment that it really doesn't matter very much. I say, "I'll go call the last shop we were in to see if it's there," and he says "It's probably here somewhere; I just need to keep organizing." The dream fades out on a happy scene of unpacking in our cheerful little house, a vision of paint colors dancing in my head . . .

*Note by Kate: I changed the original dream when I reworked it here, by adding power (problem solving, communication, patience, a positive "growth" mind set) where before there was powerlessness (whining, rage, revenge, and failure to communicate) all around. In other words, I turned fear and anger into courage and action.

I also realized that things don't have to be perfect for us to be happy. And strength comes in surprising ways. The dream in its new form leaves me with a wonderful feeling of the incompleteness of life (we're still in a mess, the bag is still missing,), which is really completeness in disguise!

SUMMARY

Now that you've learned some tools with which to uncover the wisdom within your dreams, play with these tools to discover what your dreams have to tell you. Remember, there is no right and wrong way to do them—just use them in a manner that is meaningful to you and that touches your heart. In this kind of work, it's your heart that will awaken your mind, not the other way around. I invite you to listen to what your heart has to say.

Next, if you are ready for more adventure, turn to Part Three of this book and find out what happens when you treat your life as a waking dream.

PART THREE

The Waking Dream

CHAPTER TWELVE

Exploring Your Life as a Dream

UNCOVERING THE WAKING DREAM

I encourage you to think of dreaming as something that happens both when you're asleep and when you're awake. While you sleep, your inner wisdom reveals itself to you through dream images; once you awaken, your inner wisdom shows itself to you through the events and relationships that appear in your everyday life.

Why can you see inner wisdom reflected in the events of your daily life? Because inner wisdom is always alive within you, and you act, together with the rest of the universe, to create your every day experiences. Both the wise, loving part of you and the more contracted parts of you send out intentions that act like magnetic beams of energy, attracting certain people and events into your life. By taking a calm, careful look at what is going on with these people and events, you can see a reflection of what's going on inside yourself. You can start healing those parts of yourself that are creating experiences you don't like and settle more fully into those parts that are already strong, beautiful, and ready to invite miracles your way.

To see this "waking dream," the connection between the different events that are happening in your life, try looking carefully at what's taking place around you. Feel the depths of what's going on. Pay attention to any patterns in your experience, noting any similar or strongly contrasting events or emotions that appear during your waking hours. Notice the ways in which external events mirror some part of the vast universe that's alive and pulsing within you.

Then, if you like, you can do some of the waking dream exercises in this chapter. Or you can just breathe deeply and ask your heart questions like: Why was that snake wriggling across my path just then? Can I feel something wanting to wriggle free within myself? Why did that excruciatingly slow-moving car pull out in front of me at that instant? Is there something I really want to learn right now about slowing down? And why did three different people talk to me about weddings today? Is there a part of me that wants to make a unified, wholehearted commitment to something in my own life right now?

If you asked yourself the underlying meaning of all your experiences, you'd probably drive yourself mad. Your brain would become cluttered with way too many ideas.

Yet, you can retain your sanity and still stay aware of the waking dream, by sensing the rhythm, the flow, and the connecting threads that pass through all that happens with you. Then when you feel the strong impulse to do so, you can ask your deepest self why certain experiences are strewn across your path. The more you can give yourself permission to feel the waking dream, the more easily you can converse with the luminous intelligence that anchors your earthly journey.

As I mentioned before, this chapter contains all the tools you need to explore your life as a waking dream. (Many of these are the same tools you'd use to explore a dream you experienced during sleep.) I invite you to play with them and uncover, as fully as you can, the endlessly creative dream that is your life.

A QUICK GUIDE TO USING
WAKING DREAM EXERCISES

Here's some advice about which waking dream exercises to use in different situations:

- When you are seeking a deeper understanding of what is happening in your day, use: Day Dream, Specific Event Dream, Day Dream Dance, or Inner Wise Woman/Medicine Man Dialogue

- When you are seeking a broader view of the lessons you are learning in your life right now, use: Day Dream, Specific Event Dream, Day Dream Dance, Dream Dance for Integrating Different Parts of Your Life, Inner Wise Woman/Medicine Man Dialogue, or Great Spirit Dialogue

- When you feel enveloped in certain emotions that are uncomfortable, use: Strong Emotion Dialogue, Inner Wisewoman/Medicine Man Dialogue, Heart Dialogue

- When you are yearning for a certain experience or possession that you feel is not available to you for some reason, use: Dialogue With Something You Want that is Not Presently Available

- When a relationship has ended, but you still long for it, use: Relationship Dialogue, Inner Wisewoman/Medicine Man Dialogue, Heart Dialogue

- When there's something you want to do but you feel afraid to do it, use: Strong Emotion Dialogue, Inner Wisewoman/Medicine Man Dialogue, Heart Dialogue, Dream Dance to Help You Realize a Goal

- When you've had an unpleasant interaction with someone, use: Relationship Dialogue

- When you are either contemplating a major change in your life or have already made it and are feeling a little uncertain or very freaked out, use: Major Life Change Dialogue

- When your body is achy, ill, or exhibiting some other sign of imbalance, use: Body Dream

- When you need to make a choice about something, use: Dream Dance to Help You Make a Choice

- When you have done something you regret, use: Inner Wise Woman/Medicine Man Dialogue, Heart Dialogue

- When you feel pulled in more than one direction in your life or when you need help integrating more than one passion, idea, or activity, use: Dream Dance for Integrating Different Parts of Your Life

· When you'd like to create more financial abundance in your life, use: Money Dialogue

· When you are not digesting well, are unhappy with your eating patterns, or want to know the effects that certain foods have on your body, use: Food Dialogue

· When you have a new goal that you'd like to see manifest, use: Dream Dance to Help You Realize a Goal, Inner Wise Woman/Medicine Man Dialogue, Great Spirit Dialogue

· When you feel stuck, when there's something you're having trouble letting go of or allowing in, or when you need help in any way, use: Inner Wise Woman/Medicine Man Dialogue, Heart Dialogue, Great Spirit Dialogue

· When you are feeling two or more of the above, give yourself a hug, and then use: Heart Dialogue or the Great Spirit Dialogue (then follow some of the specific suggestions above)

CHAPTER THIRTEEN

Basic Waking Dream Exercises

DAY DREAM

Use this exercise with a day in your waking life to learn what "the outside world" can teach you about what's going on "inside" of you.

To begin, write down the story of a day in your waking life. Pay particular attention to any unusual events that took place, little details that stood out, and any strong feelings that arose in you.

Then choose one of the tools from Part Two to explore this day as if it were a dream. I usually use the Themes exercise when I am exploring a whole day. Sometimes, I use it in combination with Dream Dance, which I do with three characters from my day. If you'd just like to explore one incident during your day, I suggest you turn to the Specific Event Dream exercise described a little later in this chapter.

First Example: Nancy's Day

Nancy explored a day in her waking life by using the Themes exercise.

My friend Aaron asked me if I wanted to go to breakfast and I said, 'I am short on cash this month and I've learned to say yes to free food—so, yes!' That brought up memories of how, in the past, it was the other way around and I was the one offering to pay for his meal. (Financial thought.) Then at breakfast Aaron tried to check his bank balance and his phone died. (Reflecting more fear of lack?) Only when the bill came and he paid with his debit card would he find out if he had enough in his account to pay for our meal. (Again, fear of lack.) His card worked and the world was right again.

I started my workday. Today, I was filling in at my old job. I was doing this for a number of reasons, but one was financial. (Fear of lack.) As I drove over there, and later when I drove home, my mind often drifted to financial concerns—i.e., I'd like to buy such and such, but I can wait on that . . . I wish I had the cash to buy what I really want for dinner . . . I wonder if I can do/get that this week or if I'll have to wait for the next paycheck, etc.

Another smaller (?) theme in my day was how love, affection, and concern kept coming to me. Aaron "took care of breakfast" and afterwards, he hugged me. Bradley came up to me in the restaurant and gave me a hug and asked how I was doing. Deb at FM said she'd miss me when I left, but that I could leave whenever I needed to without concern about the timing. Several favorite customers came into my workplace and offered me hugs and meaningful conversation."

Title for this Day: Lack of Financial Abundance

I think what I learned from examining my day and its themes was just how much energy I devote to the idea of not having enough money. It is always a surprise to notice the frequency of the same thought. I knew that lack of abundance was running through my mind, but it was startling to see how often. It had spread like a wildfire through my consciousness and was chewing up possibilities for positive experiences. Once I realized this, I knew that I had a choice to either take action or ignore what was going on.

Wanting to take action, I started to interject positive affirmations into my stream of thoughts whenever I heard myself repeat a "lack" statement.

So, what does this theme really mean to me? Lack of abundance . . . I was raised in the middle class, but my home life was driven by my mother's belief in lack. She had been one of seven children raised during the Great Depression and was always anxious that she didn't have enough, or that what she did have would be taken away. I grew up thinking that way too. The theme has emerged and faded throughout my life.

My divorce brought it forward again. I received a settlement but, after a year or so, I realized that my income didn't support my lifestyle and I made changes. One of the "outside" changes I made was to create a budget outline. I realized from the "inside" that I had enough, that I was always taken care of, and that money would show up when I needed it. Immediately after I affirmed those ideas, Spirit sent me an angel of a roommate who fixed things around the house and gifted me with cash whenever he felt I needed it.

Last year, I decided to quit my job and go off on my own. That year seemed to be an opportunity to see and live out some old thought patterns. What came up very largely were my beliefs in lack. Suddenly, I was making almost half the amount of money I had been making, and my plan to build a home business fell apart. I knew I was scrambling to pay bills and cutting down on food and anything else I could. But until I did this exercise, I didn't realize how much of my life and thinking revolved around the idea of not having enough. This exercise showed me how much of this particular day was affected by thoughts that there was a shortage of money. I could hardly turn around or go any-where without this kind of scarcity thinking coming into the decisions I was making. Even going to breakfast with Aaron brought ideas of "lack" forward. He mirrored my fear that money was scarce when he couldn't get through on his phone to make sure that his previous deposit had gone through. I worried that there wasn't enough in his ac-count to pay for our meal and that I might have to pay it. So this sense of scarceness cut my positive experience of a free meal down to fear.

This exercise and my reflections on it really helped me to begin turning things around. I started by verbalizing gratitude for what I did have. When I paid my bills, I ex-pressed gratitude that I could pay them. I felt grateful for the sunshine . . . birds . . . spring.

Then the opportunity to work part time at my old job came up. Same pay and benefits. After that, the job expanded into a full-time job. I still have a few hiccups now with "lack," but for the most part, I am back on the road of having my bills covered and feeling that life is looking brighter once again.

The other theme in my day was the one of receiving love. I kept getting unexpected reminders of being loved. This always makes me smile and warms my heart when it happens. It is so easy to get lost in this illusionary world and forget that love is what we are and that the universe is full of love. It is so wonderful to get a "warm fuzzy" that reminds us of our divine nature. When we remember our divinity, then insecurities, low self-esteem, and doubt all fade. Even if those feelings fade for just for a minute, we get to be one with love and the entire universe!

Second Example: Ana Lora's Morning
Note: About six years ago I explored the following morning in my waking life using the Themes exercise.

I am helping my oldest son Canyon, who is nine as I write this, get ready for school. We are late. Before we go, I try to help him brush his teeth and hair.

Physical tasks such as these have not been easy for Canyon to master in this lifetime. At school, they call him a special needs child. What I see is that his vast spirit is settling into his body very slowly; only as he starts to trust that he is safe here in this world does he agree to participate. Though many other children are reluctant to do these kinds of every day tasks, too, he has more difficulty coordinating his body movements and staying focused on his actions than many children his age. He regularly gets sidetracked, making up songs or imaginative stories, and he lets his hands go completely slack.

I try to let him do as much as possible on his own, patiently and gently helping him to refocus. When I am feeling serene within myself, I can understand his reluctance to be present while doing something so repetitive. It is something I have often experienced myself. But on this day, I am feeling a little stressed, and I am not residing in the center of my own wisdom.

So I hurry him along roughly and I am a little harsh both with my words and my touch. Canyon reacts immediately, crying out that I am mean and he would rather be with his father. These days he does not tolerate the smallest lack of consideration from me, but he also seems to forgive me quickly.

I am not so quick to forgive myself. Realizing how insensitive I was acting, I feel a sour, unpleasant feeling enter my stomach and creep up to my throat. As I take Canyon to school, I feel horribly guilty and sad that I have treated him unkindly, especially on the day that he is returning to his father's house. Yet, he kisses me sweetly when he says goodbye at the door to his classroom and asks me to remind his father, who will pick him up later in the day, to bring his toy "Wolfie" to school. I say I will and then I wave goodbye and scoot off to get his younger brother Forest ready for his school.

As I make Forest's lunch, I add in a "slug"—a garlic- and salt-covered bagel. When I'm done, we play a game together called "Wild Animal Safari" in our remaining time. Then he puts his toy kitty in his backpack and I take him to school.

Upon arriving there, I greet many of the forty or so children who go to school there by name. I think that if I can acknowledge each of them as individuals and help them to feel more visible in any way, I want to try and do that. I notice that each child whom I greet by name brightens at that moment and becomes more animated and alive.

When Forest and I enter his classroom, we find out that his teacher has been unexpectedly delayed and is going to arrive late on this day, so I hang out with the kids until she gets there. Then I give my son a big kiss and take off.

Driving home in my car, I start feeling sad again about my earlier interactions with Canyon. The fact that he is leaving for his father's house today makes my sadness about our conflict balloon into something large, and attached with all kinds of ribbons of guilt. My shame and grief grow until I burst into tears.

At that moment, I look up and see a peregrine falcon landing on a telephone wire. She lands a little clumsily and almost looks as if she's going to topple over. But she adjusts herself quickly and regains her balance.

Title for My Morning: Life's Balancing Act

Lots of animals are showing up today in my daydream— "Wolfie," the "slug" bagel in Forest's lunch, the safari game, Forest's toy kitty, and the falcon. Animals remind me of breath and fur and warmth . . . they make me think of movement and aliveness . . . of energy pulsing within the body. Animals are vibrant teachers because they trust their instincts and intuition. They stay relaxed unless they need to respond to an immediate challenge. They do not hang onto stressful thoughts from the past or project worries into the future. Nor do they seem to "space out" for long periods in the way that humans do. Animals are here and now.

I can learn from the animals by relaxing into this breath and this moment. I can also forgive both my son and myself for having times when we don't want to fully engage in this world. It's okay that we both feel a little afraid or clumsy at times.

The awareness that I have not been as kind to my son as I could have been is a hard thing to face. Yet, I can see that and grow, setting my intention to be kinder to him the next time. I can also let go of guilt and appreciate myself more fully for the kindness I did show to others on this day—to the children and the teacher, at my younger son's school, who was late.

I did not know, when I first saw the falcon, what she was showing me in this waking dream. I watched this powerful creature, who seems so at home in wind, air, and ethers, trying to make a landing on a thin wire on the earth, and I did not see what her experience had to do with me. Now, I realize that both she and I were discovering that sometimes there's the finest line, the tiniest difference, between responding fully to what lies before us and just responding most of the way. Sometimes, we forget to use some significant part of who we are in the present moment, so we lose our balance and topple. We get impatient with someone we love. We speak or act harshly. We trip over our own feet.

What my waking dream showed me is that even powerful, beautiful, skilled creatures like this falcon can make a mistake, stumble, and almost fall over. But she shifts quickly, and just like that regains her balance.

I believe she is telling me that I can do this, too. Yet, how? As I pause and consider this, what comes to me is that it would help to breath deeply, look within to discover the real source of the stress I was feeling at the moment that I reacted unkindly, and offer myself more compassion. Maybe if I listen more to myself, loosen up a little on my own self-doubts, and open to the true tenderness that lies within my heart, I can find my balance once again.

BODY DREAM

This tool allows you to converse with the subtle intelligence of your own body so that you can find out what your body needs, especially when it is sick or injured.

To begin, close your eyes and choose a body part that feels as though it would like to speak with you. Then turn to the Dialoguing exercise in Part Two and talk with this body part exactly as if it were a dream character. If some part of your body is aching, put your awareness right in the center of the ache and answer the Dialoguing questions from that perspective.)

First Example: Janel's Experience

Recently, the right neck/shoulder/arm/hand area of my body has been experiencing a lot of discomfort. I work full-time as a bookkeeper, so this has been interfering with my work. From time to time, I'm not really sure I want to be a bookkeeper, but I am fearful of changing careers, because it seems it would have such a big impact on my family. This is the dialoguing I did with that sore area.

Janel's Dialogue

Janel: How are you feeling?

Sore Area: I feel as though there is something extra in me. It is filling up space that needs to be more open. There is a specific spot of tension. It feels like there is some sort of adjustment needed in the alignment of the shoulder position and how it interacts with a nerve flowing down your arm, though your elbow, and into your hand. Those are the physical sensations.

   On the emotional level, I am feeling crowded and irritated. I am frustrated that you are not taking care of me and that you haven't found a way to make me feel better. You are not giving me enough attention.

Janel: What do you have to teach me?

Sore Area: It is important for you to take the time for yourself, and to give yourself things that you need even if your mind says that you don't really "need" them. It is important for you to let go of comparing your needs to other peoples and thinking that because they don't require something, you don't either. You are you, and you can trust that you can have what is essential to your wellbeing. You don't have to shut off your awareness of your needs because you fear "there is not enough." The universe will support you.

Janel: What can you tell me about bringing more love into my life?

Sore Area: By giving yourself what you need, you are validating your spirit. When you validate your spirit, you release more energy and love into your life.

Second Example: Nancy's Experience

My right calf is drawing my attention because it is painful and tight in a certain spot on the outside of the leg. There is a lot of tightness. When I go deeper than the physical pain I feel tears. Tears because it hurts and because my relationship just ended; tears that the future is now a solo path instead of a joint path.

Nancy's Dialogue

Nancy: Right calf, what do you have to tell me?

Calf: Take time for emotional expression. You need to love yourself more in general—especially now, when the ending of the relationship is still so new.

Nancy: Anything else?

Calf: Until you allow yourself to feel love moving through you, like the love you felt when spending time with your boyfriend, and until your whole being resonates with that sensation, the pain will not release completely. Stretching will help you reduce the pain and make you more comfortable, but releasing your tears and flooding your body with love will make it whole again.

Third Example: Michael's Experience

I had some sort of intense stomach/intestinal discomfort that caused me to feel gaseous and nauseous. During this time, I had several brief bouts of vomiting and diarrhea.

Afterwards, I decided to do the Dialoguing exercise with my stomach.

Michael's Dialogue

Michael: Stomach, how are you feeling?

Stomach: Tight, clenched, worried, afraid. I've been trying to protect you by limiting what comes in. Since I've been overprotecting you recently. I've been out of balance and that made you susceptible to this illness.

Michael: What part of me are you?

Stomach: A part that's strong, but also leery of the unknown. A part that's uneasy and feeling a lot of stress right now, especially around work and finances. Also, a part that is stuck in old patterns.

Michael: What do you need?

Stomach: I need to breathe as if long ocean waves are moving through me. I need to relax deeply.

Michael: What do you have to tell me?

Stomach: Well, on a physical level, you need to cultivate a loose, easy way of breathing. No force. Gentle flow in, gentle flow out. You also need to be easy and gentle with yourself on other levels.

Beyond that, there comes a time in the spiritual evolution of every human being when trust becomes of utmost importance if you are going to keep moving forward. Trust the things that you know are true, trust the love that surrounds you, trust that you will be supported in following your bliss.

You need to take a leap of faith. Every evolving person reaches this point. Are you willing to believe completely in love, miracles, and healing? To move into the fullness of your potential, you must trust. There's no way around this. No shortcut.

Michael: Is there anything else you'd like me to know?

Stomach: Allow more warmth in your life. Feel complete acceptance of who you are. Seek to know yourself as honestly as you can. Recognize what you need, and accept yourself completely. When you love yourself and feel completely worthy of love, it will be easier for you to recognize support that is available to you from the outside world. You can surrender and let go of the fear that makes you feel the need to defend yourself at your own expense. Love is here.

SPECIFIC EVENT DREAM

Write down a description of a walk you took, a business meeting, class, or celebration you attended, or an encounter with another person, animal, or object that strongly affected you. Then choose one of the exercises from Part Two and do that exercise with this part of your waking life experience, treating the event exactly as if it were a dream. Often the Point of View, Dialoguing, or Dream Body exercise works particularly well with this one.

First Example: Karen's Encounter with a Snake

Last week, while my friend Marilyn and I were taking a hike in the redwoods, we came across a snake stretched out across the trail. At first glance, I was excited to see it. But it didn't move and when I examined it more closely, I wondered if it were dead. Then I noticed a slight indentation in its back and in its jaw, which was remaining open. I suspect that a mountain biker rushing down this trail had run over the snake while it was sunning itself. It had probably been lying there, warming its cold body, feeling peaceful and content, and then, as quickly as it was aware of an oncoming threat, it was smashed by a person who was oblivious to his environment.

I tried to do my best by picking up the snake to place her in a more private and respectable place. Then I saw her move slightly. She was still alive!

Oh, my heart ached. Was she in pain? Was I inflicting even more pain by trying to help her? What was the best thing I could do for her? I felt helpless.

Looking into her eyes, I tried to sense what she wanted me to do. She wanted me to leave her to rest and die in peace. But my friend Marilyn suggested that we take the snake to a place near water in case she wanted to drink. Can a snake drink when her jaw is stuck open? I didn't really stop to listen to myself, or to the snake. I only paid attention to Marilyn, because she's been an animal rescuer of sorts, and is a lover of nature.

So I wrapped her in Marilyn's jacket and carried her a long way in search of a stream and some sunshine. Yet, I worried the whole way. Did being curled up hurt her if her spine was broken? Would it have been better just to leave her alone to die? Why had I just taken Marilyn's advice?

We finally found a sunny spot under a log and by a stream, which was ideal for the moment. But the sun would move and, eventually, she would be in the cold again. By carrying her there, had I given her only more pain and fear in the last moments of her life? Would she have been able to survive, even in the most favorable of conditions?

I hoped then that another beast of nature, perhaps a hawk, would find her and put her out of her misery. Providing life for another seemed like the best possible outcome.

Thinking of her now, I project feelings of fear, confusion, and pain onto her. And I am reminded of the circumstances when my mother was dying. After all of the efforts my family and I made to ensure that my mother's passage would be peaceful and painless, she died gasping for air, her eyes wide with fear, because of the neglect of the night-shift caretaker.

I will always ask myself whether I did the best I could in both of these situations. Were their fates out of my hands as I attempted to provide them with peaceful deaths, or did I not do enough? It feels as though I can never do enough, but it is as it should be and I need to let it all go.

Karen's Dialogue with the Snake

Karen: My biggest concern is that I might have hurt you by trying to help you. Did I hurt you?

Snake: I was frightened and confused. Yet, don't worry about having hurt me. Your concern about pain, although real, does not matter. Your intentions were good. What happened, happened; you need to let go. This is your challenge and your lesson.

Karen: Good intentions or not, I can't just let go. I took responsibility for your life situation, and I continue to question whether or not I failed at helping you. Perhaps, you would have been happier drifting silently into death on the trail upon which you were hurt. I listened to the advice of another. I didn't listen to you. I didn't listen to myself.

Snake: But now you are listening to yourself, and that is good.

Karen: Okay, I know that I need to listen more to myself. I understand, in my mind, that I need to learn to let go. I hear your words, but I hate the idea of hurting you. I see you as mystery and power. You are magic to me. You are good. I don't like the idea of causing you unnecessary pain and suffering.

Snake: You worry too much about others. Your own mystery, power, magic, and good is to be your focus. Be good to yourself and in so doing you will do well for others. You already know this. Yet, you don't listen.

Karen: I am stubborn and hardheaded at times. What you are saying is difficult for me to believe. I was taught to take care of others, and I feel as though I fail at times.

Snake: Why are you worried about failing? You teach your children that when they make a mistake it is an opportunity to learn. Is this any different?

Karen: I guess I feel in doubt, because I don't know if what I did was the right or wrong thing to do. I would have felt the same if I had left you on the trail.

Snake: So it is not knowing that is bothering you.

Karen: How can I learn without knowing what is right?

Snake: Perhaps this is an opportunity to learn that you need not always to know. You do not need to determine whether your actions were right or wrong. Instead of worrying about that, look at what you have already learned from this experience. You know that you want to listen more to yourself. You know that you want to let go of what is past. You know that you want to better respect your own needs. You know that you want to be able to forgive yourself.

Karen: That's a full plate.

Snake: When you look at yourself, one hopes to find a full plate, not an empty one.

Karen: What part of myself are you?

Snake: I talk from your heart, yet I am that which you call mystery and power, magic and good. I am the mystery and power, magic, and good within you. When you acknowledge and honor me as part of yourself, you will be able to love yourself more and thus bring more love into your life.

Second Example: Ana Lora's Walk

I stand at my window and look out. A big storm of heavy rains and wild winds has just passed. Now, the world seems gray and quiet. I decide to go out and walk up into the woods that are only a block away.

After clomping out the door and down my driveway in my hiking boots, I turn onto the street and see the old, gentle golden retriever that lives nearby, waddling up the road not far ahead of me. I know she is probably not aware that I am coming up behind her, because I don't think she hears very well. When I pass by, I give her a wide berth to keep from scaring her.

My street is a busy one. Cars are swooshing past us both at a fast rate of speed. I experience a moment of worry for this sweet creature, but she seems to be okay. So I smile back at her and walk on. She keeps toddling along slowly as I take faster strides up to the woods.

Once I have climbed the stairs by the water tower and have entered the tall stands of evergreens, I take big gulps of the damp, green air—almost as if I thought I would never breathe again. I check behind the large redwood where I hide my walking stick. It is there as always, and all wet from the storm that just passed.

Grasping my stick in my hand, I follow the path up into the green and brown world I know so well. It's a world that feels like home to me. In every direction, I see evidence of the recent storm. Branches litter the ground in mighty jumbles. Everything is soggy. The path itself has become thick, brown goo that clings to my boots with every step I take.

When I reach the first fork in my path, I leave the main trail behind and take the narrow trail that climbs steeply uphill. As I ascend through the trees, I feel my breath moving through me like a strong wind, and I realize how much I need to feel that. I pause for a moment, chest heaving, and then press on.

After climbing for a while, I start to get sweaty. At this point I am painted with mud and decorated with twigs. I decide to turn around and, just at that moment, I hear bagpipes playing. I stumble on a little longer, hoping to see the musician, but I never do. The melody weaves its way through the forest, but I don't see who is doing the playing.

So I turn and tromp back down, down, down and out of my woods. By the big redwood, I set my stick in its' spot and then head down to the road.

This time, as I step out onto the street, I notice that the long fence that previously hid the backyard directly across from me has come down in the storm. A month before, around Christmas, I heard a big dog snarling behind that barrier. He must have been visiting, because there is no dog there now. Instead, there is just some old fallen wood and a sense of quiet release.

Leaving this scene behind, I move on down the street and past the horse pasture. I see a tall, regal-looking horse standing there, regarding me solemnly out of large black eyes. As I continue to look at him, he suddenly starts pee-ing! I am so surprised by the unexpected golden cascade that I start laughing out loud.

I am still smiling as I turn into my own driveway and head back to my warm house.

From Old Dog Ambling Up the Street
Point of View

Note: In this next example, I decide to do the Point of View exercise from Part Two with many of the characters from my waking dream.

I am old, my sight is dimmed, my hearing is gone. I cannot move quickly. Any anger and defensiveness I once may have felt are gone, and all that is left is my old, gentle core—only what is essential remains for me.

Ana Lora sees me like an old friend, and I am. I move through this world as well as I can and let the rest go. I don't worry about anything. I know that something in the heart of all things protects me, guides me, and watches over me. You might think I am endangered in this fast moving world, but I am not. I am protected. I have my place. Whatever truly belongs here on this earth is protected. There are no accidents. I will not dissolve and leave this planet until I am completely done with my life here. I allow myself to relax, and you can, too, dear Ana Lora. There is nothing to fear here.

From Bagpipes
Point of View

We are the faraway music, the elven melody that you hear, the song of the soul and of nature. We call to you, leading you forth, and helping you to find your place in this world. As you respond to this ancient song, your heart comes home. It finds its own peace, and you know there is nothing more to prove. The truths that you know become clearer and stronger. All you need to do is open your heart and listen, Ana Lora.

From Newly Fallen Fence
Point of View

I am open. I have come down. The barriers inside me are dislodging, releasing, and disintegrating. I am losing my desire to hold things in or keep them out. I am letting go of tightness, of the need to keep up any kind of front. I am moving toward allowing, and you are, too, my friend.

I am old. I can come down, open, and make way for the new. This is the natural way—this letting go, this surrender to what iIs. I am gone the way of all nature.

The angry, territorial dog that was briefly inside me has gone, too. Nothing fearsome is going to come lunging out at you or others when I, or you, let go. You do not need to worry about anyone getting hurt if you relax your strong concentration on self-control, dear one. It's time to stop trying to "fit yourself into" your ideas of what is good or responsible, it's time to stop monitoring your behavior moment to moment for its rightness or wrongness. Trust yourself more. Trust what wants to come out from inside of you. The real you is a gift you can give to yourself and others. Allow it to flow out.

It's time for me to release old barriers and open; and it's time for you, Ana Lora, to release and open all the way, too.

From Horse that Is Peeing
Point of View

I am big and strong and free. Even though I live a tame life, there is an element of wildness in me. I pee for Ana Lora to emphasize how natural it is to let go. I help her to remember (in a humorous way that delights her) to surrender to the deepest calls of her own nature.

From the Forest
Point of View

Ana Lora feels this yearning to be with me, to breathe in all that I am, all the way down to my core. She wants to wrap herself in the greenness of my leaves and grass and brownness of my bark, branches, and squishy mud. She yearns for my cool, clear air, the sounds of my twittering birds, and the steady humming of ancient life that moves through my trees and me. I am so alive.

I embrace Ana Lora completely. She is at home with me. She knows that love is simple when she is with me. We see each other, we know each other, and we love each other. Our hearts join together effortlessly. Without her mind realizing it, her heart has been aching for this communion—craving it—like someone who has been thirsty for far too long.

When Ana Lora physically leaves me, she is not the same. She takes me back with her, feeling me inside of her. It is partly my strength that runs through her legs, my voice that weaves its' soothing tones into her voice, my light that shines out through her eyes. I have helped Ana Lora to dissolve everything she doesn't need, to surrender to what is true. The more she can let down her inner walls and fences, the more she can experience the gentleness, the strength, and the peacefulness that is the core of who she is . . . and the essence of all creation.

CHAPTER FOURTEEN

Waking Dream Dances

DAY DREAM DANCE

Choose three characters that played a significant role in your life on any given day. (Remember that a character can be any living being, object, or part of the landscape.) Now, turn to the Dream Dance exercise (page 103) with those three characters.

DREAM DANCE FOR INTEGRATING DIFFERENT PARTS OF YOUR LIFE.

Choose two or three parts of your life that you would like to see fitting together more easily. These could include romance, work, family life, friendship, kindness to your body, creative self-expression, school, alone time, etc. Treat each of these areas as a dream character. If you like you can create a symbol in your mind for each one, such as a red rose for romance, a desk for work, or the living room couch for family life. Then turn to the Dream Dance exercise with these two or three characters, finding ways that these different parts of your life can flow together in a unified dance.

DREAM DANCE TO HELP YOU MAKE A CHOICE

When you are trying to choose between several options—a number of places to live, multiple avenues of study, more than one offer of employment—this exercise can help you step out of the endless circles of indecision you may be traveling in and help you step into deeper clarity.

To do this exercise, find a nice open space where you can move freely and don't have to worry about bumping into furniture. If you like, you can ask a friend to witness what you are doing and record their impressions.

Now, close your eyes and focus on how your first option makes you feel. Try doing some physical movements to express these feelings. Add sounds if you like. Keep experimenting with movement and sound until you feel that you have explored all your responses to this choice. Then pause and breathe deeply, keeping your eyes closed. When you are ready, explore the next option or two in the same way.

Once you have explored all three choices, dance from one option to the next fairly quickly, feeling what changes in you with each option. Do this cycle several times.

After exploring all your choices, take a moment to write down whatever impressions came to you during the exercise. How did each option feel in your body? Was there one that felt the best? Were there strengths or advantages in the other options that you still might want to incorporate in your life in a new, creative way, even though they might not be your main choice?

If someone else has been witnessing this exercise, you can share your experiences with them, and then ask them what their impressions were.

You can also try dialoguing with the different alternatives. To do this, create a mental image that represents each option and then dialogue with it as if it were a dream character. For instance, if you were trying to choose between several places to live, you might want to visualize the different houses or apartments and talk to each of those places. If you were attempting to decide whether to major in biology or art, you might want to imagine a living cell and a paintbrush and then dialogue with each of these characters.

DREAM DANCE TO HELP YOU REALIZE A GOAL

Write down a goal that you have in any given area: work, finances, health, romance, friendship, home environment, family, creative expression, personal boundary setting, education, travel, etc.

Find a nice, quiet space in which to move freely. Begin by focusing on where you are now in relation to this goal. What is your current situation? Explore where you are now by making different movements that reflect your present situation. Feel all the feelings that come up as you do this. Take your time.

Next, imagine that you have right now realized your heart's desire. Dance out the experience of having manifested your wish and explore how you feel about doing that. Again, use all the time you need to immerse yourself in the experience.

Now, allow yourself to feel what you did in order to move from not having achieved your heart's desire to having done so. What changed within you? What did you need to let go of? What did you need to allow in? If you like, you can try the above two steps again, paying attention to the changes that occur as you move from where you are right now to where you'd like to be.

After this, return to the experience of "where you are right now" in relation to this goal, but very slowly begin releasing what you need to release, and allowing in what you need to allow in, in order to create your goal. Keep going until you are again feeling what it feels like to have fully achieved your intention. Really immerse yourself in this experience for as long as you like. When you feel complete, stop and either write down your impressions or share them out loud if you are working with a partner.

If you would like any more help in reaching your heart's desire, do either the Strong Emotion Dialogue (page 171) with your fear and doubt, or the Inner Wise Woman/Medicine Man Dialogue (page 172) and ask the wisest part of your being questions about how to attain this strong wish.

CHAPTER FIFTEEN

Waking Dream Dialogues

STRONG EMOTION DIALOGUE: DIALOGUE WITH YOUR DOUBT, FEAR, ANGER, SADNESS, JOY, OR OTHER FEELINGS

Whenever you are experiencing doubt, fear, sadness, anger, confusion, worry, nervous excitement, deep desire, unbridled joy, or some other strong feeling, you may want to turn to the Dialoguing exercise (page 88) and dialogue with that feeling as if it were a dream character. If you choose, you can envision a symbol for this feeling: a thick, gray fog for sadness, a snorting bull for anger, or a soaring bird for joy, for example, and then dialogue with this symbol as if it were a dream character. Find out why this feeling is part of your experience and what it has to teach you. You can also notice whether this feeling changes once you have had a dialogue with it.

RELATIONSHIP DIALOGUE:
DIALOGUE WITH A PERSON YOU KNOW

When you are having a conflict with someone, or when you would just like to deepen a relationship, turn to the Dialoguing exercise and imagine dialoguing with that person as if he or she were a dream character. In the upcoming days, notice whether this dialogue has either altered or enhanced your relationship in any way.

INNER WISE WOMAN
OR MEDICINE MAN DIALOGUE

Imagine that there is a wise, old, powerful woman or man within you. What might she or he look, sound, or feel like? Envision this being as fully as you can. Then whenever you feel small, vulnerable, weak, stuck, confused, unhappy, or somewhat limited in your view of your experience, try talking to this wise, loving, and compassionate part of yourself. Use some of the questions suggested in the Dialoguing exercise to open communication, and then ask this part of yourself advice on any area of your life.

MAJOR LIFE CHANGE DIALOGUE

Whenever you make or consider making a large change in your circumstances, talking with the part of your being that is initiating the shift can help change to happen more easily and intentionally. You can either try talking to this part of your being directly (without a visual aid) or you can envision a symbol for it. For instance, you might imagine the part of you that wants to end a relationship as a wounded child, or as a wise old grandmotherly person . . . the part of you that wants to move to another town as a giant dancer or a migrating whale . . . the part of you that wants to quit your 9 to 5 job so that you can have greater "freedom" as a wild mustang or an accomplished artist. Once you have decided which way you'd like to speak with the motivating force behind the change you are making, turn to Part Two and do the Dialoguing exercise.

YOUR HEART DIALOGUE

Whenever you want to talk with your heart, you can turn to the Dialoguing exercise (page 88) and begin a dialogue, treating your heart as if it were a dream character. You can ask your heart anything. Ask it to help you understand something you are feeling, or something that's happening in your life. Then inquire about what it would like you to learn right now, what it would like you to do, and what it can tell you about *you*!

FOOD DIALOGUE

Whenever you are unhappy about your eating habits, or wonder what effect a certain food might have on you, turn to the Dialoguing exercise and use the general guidelines given there to start a dialogue. Ask this food how it feels, what it has to give you, what it cannot offer you, when you need to eat it or not eat it, and how else you can nurture yourself when it would be better for you not to eat it. Also ask it what part of you it reflects, and what it can tell you about inviting more love into your life.

MONEY DIALOGUE

Whenever you'd like to create more financial abundance in your life, turn to the Dialoguing exercise and speak with money as if it were a dream character. In addition to using the questions listed there, you can also ask money how you can strengthen your relationship with it, what you need to do to allow more of it into your life, what part of you it reflects right now, how it would like to have more fun with you, and what it has to tell you about love.

DIALOGUE WITH SOMETHING YOU WANT THAT IS NOT PRESENTLY AVAILABLE

I came up with this one when I really, really wanted to do an end-of-the-season backpack trip into the mountains and a serious head cold prevented me from doing so. I was *so* disappointed! Then I decided to dialogue with the mountains I wanted to visit. Once I did this, three things happened. I deeply experienced the mountains' steady presence inside of me, I started feeling incredibly happy, and the desperate yearning to physically go to the mountains went away!

To do this exercise yourself, dialogue with the object of your desire. Find out what it knows, what it has to teach you, what part of you it reflects, and what it can tell you about cultivating more love in your life.

GREAT SPIRIT DIALOGUE

Whenever you like, you can speak directly with that distilled loving essence we call Spirit, God, Goddess, The Source, Buddha, Krishna, Allah, Love, and All That Is. You can imagine a symbol for this awareness, or speak with it directly. Close your eyes and feel yourself in the presence of this awareness. Take your time with this. Then ask this presence what it would most like to tell you right now. After you've received an answer, ask any specific questions you have about some area of your life, general questions about your life goals and purpose, and anything else you wish to know! Use the Dialoguing exercise if you need further inspiration.

THE SKY IS THE LIMIT DIALOGUE

Talk to anyone or anything in the whole cosmos as if it were a dream character. When you open your heart, the possibilities for loving dialogue are endless.

Summary

Now you have a strong set of tools for exploring what's going on below the surface of your waking life. Whenever your body is aching, your heart is troubled, or you are having difficulty choosing between several options in your life, you can use the tools here. If you need more clarity about a relationship, or an event that's taking place during your waking hours, you know you can find resources in these pages. This part of the book gives you all the information you need to understand your everyday experience in a profound way. I invite you to use these tools again and again, and see your life for the creative, ever-changing dream that it is.

PART FOUR

The Dream Circle

CHAPTER SIXTEEN

Exploring Dreams as a Group

FORMING YOUR CIRCLE

Love and support. I can think of no more powerful gifts we can offer ourselves, or each other. Can you? If you would like to share these gifts by forming a dream circle, here are some suggestions to help you get rolling.

Logistics

Group Size: I find that a group of six to eight lively, committed people is my preferred group size. More or less works too, though. Go with what you've got.

Meeting Length: I like to meet for about two and a half to three hours, if the group has six to eight people in it. This allows for ample time to do some in-depth work together and share what was learned. A smaller group, however, may not need to meet as long.

Meeting Frequency: Decide whether to meet once a week for several weeks, every other week, or once a month. My favorite is to meet every other week, because that allows me to feel strongly connected both to the work and the people in the group, without feeling as though the demand on my time is too much. Pick the format that works best for you.

Playing Follow the Leader: I suggest having a different person lead the group each week. They can pick the exercises you will do, watch the timing of everything, and help keep people on track.

Agreements

Confidentiality: Ask each member of the group to make a commitment to confidentiality. This means that you agree to keep secret anything that has happened with other group members, or that they have shared during your group meeting time. However, you remain free to share your own personal experience during your dream group meetings with anyone you like.

Respect: Ask each member of the group to make a commitment to respect, which means that you will not try and interpret dreams for anyone else in the group. Instead, you assist one another in finding the wisdom within yourselves. Listen, witness, and ask questions of others within the group as they share their dream explorations with you. Cry with them, laugh with them, or sit in stillness. If another person asks for your feedback, after exploring a dream himself or herself, you can say, "If this were my dream, I might pay attention to this . . ." or "I was wondering if the dream might be talking to you about this. How do you feel about that?"

Preparation: Individual or Group

· Ask everyone to read The Shape of Each Meeting (described on page 185–189).

· Ask each person to bring to each meeting either a dream, a day in their waking lives, or an event from their waking lives that they'd like to explore on a deeper level. Each person should choose three characters from that dream, day, or event that they'd like to work with. (You can opt to choose two characters for your first couple of meetings if you want to spend more time on each exercise.) Remember a "character" doesn't have to be a person. It might be one of your friends, but it can also be a tall fir tree, a cat, a school, a strong wind, a birthday cake, or any other part of your dream or waking experience that stands out to you for some reason.

· Request that each person bring a dream journal, a pen, and a copy of this book for reference when doing the exercises.

· If you have assigned yourselves homework (described in Ending the Meeting on page 188), bring that, too.

The Next Leader

Have the upcoming leader choose which exercises the group will be doing at your next meeting. The leader can find suggested exercises and meeting formats described in the section below, called The Shape of Each Meeting. Remember that these exercises can be done either with dreams or with waking life experiences. Individuals in the group can decide for themselves which area of experience they'd like to explore in any given week. However, if you'd all like to explore your waking dreams one week, the leader can either choose one of the regular formats listed below or one of the Waking Dream Formats (page 197–202). If you're using one of the Waking Dream Formats, make sure your group members know you'll be doing waking dream explorations at the next meeting so that they bring a waking life experience to work with.

THE SHAPE OF EACH MEETING

Here are some ideas:

Initial Check In

The leader starts your meeting by asking each person to briefly share what they are feeling and what they have learned from any homework they have done (homework is described in the Ending the Meeting section found on page 188). Once everyone has done this, the leader can then ask each person what dream or waking life experience he or she would like to explore during the meeting and what three characters they would like to work with.

The Body of the Meeting

During the body of the meeting, group members explore their three characters using whatever exercises or format the leader has chosen. The leader can let the group know how much time each person gets to do any given exercise, as I have listed the approximate amount of time needed for each exercise in the different formats.

When you read through these formats, you will find that often I suggest doing one or more exercises on an individual basis. Whenever this is so, I have written Silent/Point of View or Silent/Dialoguing, and so forth. To do an exercise in this way, have each person settle into a cozy spot in the room, open this book to the given exercise in Part Two, and do the exercise in a journal. In one of the seven-week classes I taught, group members wanted to explore all their dreams on a silent, individual basis. Only after all of their individual work was finished did they want to share what they had learned with the whole group. They did not want to do any partner exploration or a group exercise like Expanded Dream Body. Most of the time we did Silent Dialoguing with three different characters, followed by Dream Dance with all three characters. (I read Dream Dance aloud to them and did not participate myself, which is what your leader would need to do if you were following this option.)

Dialoguing combined with Dream Dance is one of the most powerful combinations you can do, so you may choose, as my group did, that those two exercises will be the focus of your time together over the course of many weeks. Different groups are different, however, so find out what style of exploration your group would like to do from week to week.

If your group wants to do partner exercises in addition to silent exercises, look for exercises with "Partners" in the title, for example: Partners/Dialoguing, or Partners/Dream Body and Dialoguing. In these instances, people in the group pair off and then find a place in the room that is not too close to the others. Each person takes a turn leading the other person through the given exercise with one dream or waking life character. After each turn is finished, the partners spend a few minutes sharing what was learned and feelings that were experienced with each other.

For exercises to be done as a whole group, look for exercises with "Leader" in the title, for instance: Leader/Dream Dance or Leader/Expanded Dream Body. Here, the current leader reads an exercise to the assembled group. When that happens, the leader can either sit out the exercise, or try it to some degree, although she or he needs to be able to stay focused on the group's needs. Even if your group wants to do a lot of individual work, I strongly recommend having the group leader guide the group through the Dream Dance exercise on a regular basis. It is a very powerful experience.

Ending the Meeting

I usually like to set aside about half an hour at the end of a meeting so that each person can share some key aspects of what she or he learned during the dream explorations. Remind everyone to be brief and share the key information they learned, rather than all the details of their experiences during the exercises—otherwise you'll be hanging out together all night!

Once you have done this, then your current leader can assign some "homework" to help each of you cultivate a regular dream exploration practice. For this, I usually ask the group to do an exercise like Dialoguing with at least two to three characters from either their dreams or waking lives.

Before you go home, someone new needs to volunteer to be the leader for the following meeting. You also need to decide if that meeting will be one of those rare occasions in which you'd all like to explore waking dreams together by following one of the formats listed in the Waking Dream Meeting Suggestions. If so, you might want to choose a format in that section while you are still together and figure out what you need to bring the next time.

If you are not following a waking dream format, then your leader can just decide before all of you get together again which of the formats from Dream Meeting Suggestions your group will do, and each of you can decide on your own, some time later, whether you'd like to explore three characters from dreams or from waking life at the next meeting.

Note: Using the formats described in Dream Meeting Suggestions, you can also work with two characters from a dream, and one from waking life, if you wish.

DREAM MEETING SUGGESTIONS

Please note that the times I list below are approximate. When you are first starting out you may need to give yourself a little more time with each exercise than you will need later on. You may even decide to take more time, initially, than what I have listed and only work with two characters. If you want to make sure you get through all the exercises listed, have your leader let everyone know when you only have a couple of minutes left with each exercise . . . and then ask people to stop at a point close to the ending time you've decided upon.

You can do one or more of these formats over the weeks that you work together. And you can use them in any particular order—although I have listed a few of the simpler ones at the beginning. Enjoy!

Dream Format 1

1. Initial check in (described above)—30 to 45 minutes.

2. The first time you do this, read over Point of View or Dialoguing—whichever one or two you've chosen to do next—and resolve together any questions you might have—5 to 10 minutes.

3. First dream character—Silent/Point of View—5 to 10 minutes; *or* Silent/Dialoguing—10 to 15 minutes.

4. Second dream character—Silent/Dialoguing—10 to 15 minutes.

5. Third dream character—Silent/Dialoguing—10 to 15 minutes.

6. Leader/Dream Dance—20 to 25 minutes.

7. Silent/Note-taking on your Dream Dance experience—5 to 10 minutes.

8. Last sharing (described above)—30 to 45 minutes.

Dream Format 2

1. Initial check in—30 minutes.

2. First dream character—Silent/Point of View or Silent/Dialoguing—5 to 15 minutes.

3. Second dream character—Partners/Dialoguing—25 to 30 minutes per person, including Dialoguing and sharing time (up to 1 hour total).

    Note: If you are doing Dialoguing as partners, one of you pretends to be your own dream character, while the other asks that character questions from the first basic list given in the Dialoguing exercise (page 88). The person being the dream character answers those questions out loud, staying in character. The last question asked should be: "Do you feel complete?"

    If the character says no, the person asking questions can go on and ask some of the optional questions from the second list given in that exercise. If the character says yes, he/she/it feels complete, you can stop the dialogue, share, and then change roles.

4. Third dream character—Leader/Dream Body—Up to 15 minutes.

5. Third dream character again—Silent/Dialoguing—10 to 15 minutes.

6. Silent/Do one of the suggestions from Creating Closure with Your Dream Explorations in Part Two—up to 15 minutes.

7. Last group sharing—30 minutes.

Dream Format 3

1. Initial check in—30 minutes.

2. First dream character—Silent/Point of View or Dialoguing—5 to 15 minutes.

3. Second dream character—Partners/Dialoguing—25 to 30 minutes per person, including sharing time—up to one hour total.

4. Third dream character—Partners/Dialoguing With a New Partner—25 to 30 minutes per person, including sharing time—up to one hour total.

5. Last Group Sharing—30 minutes.

Dream Format 4

1. Initial check in—30 minutes.

2. First dream character—Silent/Dialoguing—10 to 15 minutes.

3. Second dream character—Partners/Dream Body and Partners/Dialoguing—30 to 35 minutes per person, including sharing time—up to 70 minutes total.

    Note: Dream Body/Dialoguing with partners is done much the same way as Dialoguing, only in this case, the person "being the dream character" stays in character as you go directly from one of these exercises to the other. After you have completed both exercises, take a few minutes for personal sharing and then change roles.

4. Third dream character—Silent/Dialoguing—10 to 15 minutes.

5. Silent—Do one of the suggestions from Creating Closure with your dream explorations in Part Two— 10 to 15 minutes.

6. Last group sharing—30 minutes.

Dream Format 5

1. Initial check in—30 minutes.

2. First dream character—Silent/Point of View or Dialoguing—5 to 15 minutes.

3. Second dream character—Partners/Dialoguing—25 to 30 minutes per person, including sharing time; up to 1 hour total.

4. Third dream character—Silent/Dialoguing—5 to 15 minutes.

5. All three dream characters—Leader/Dream Dance—20-plus minutes.

6. Last group sharing—30 minutes.

Dream Format 6

1. Initial check in—30 minutes.

2. First dream character—Silent/Dialoguing—10 to 15 minutes.

3. All three characters—Partners/Dream Dance—30 to 40 minutes per person, including sharing time; up to 80 minutes total.

4. Second dream character—Silent/Point of View or Dialoguing—5 to 15 minutes.

5. Third dream character—Silent/Point of View—5 to 15 minutes.

6. Last group sharing—30 minutes.

Dream Format 7

1. Initial check in—30 minutes.

2. First dream character—Silent/Dialoguing—10 to 15 minutes.

3. Second dream character—Partners/Dialoguing—25 to 30 minutes per person, including sharing time; up to one hour total.

4. Third dream character—Silent/Dialoguing—10 to 15 minutes.

5. Leader/Expanded Dream Body—20 minutes.

6. Last group sharing—30 minutes.

Note: In this one, the leader guides you all through the Dream Body exercise with a dream character from one group member's dream. In other words, one group member volunteers to describe to the whole group a dream character she or he has been working with. Then everyone pretends to be that dream character while the leader leads the group through the Dream Body exercise. Each person gets to experience one group member's dream character at the same time that everyone else does.

I suggest that all of you make sounds and speak out loud, describing, in single words or brief phrases, the nature of your experience with this character. I also advise you to do this one with the understanding that whatever comes up reflects each group member's own experience with a given dream character: you are not attempting to interpret the original dreamer's experience with the character. When all of you engage in this exercise fully with your hearts and bodies, you will find that each of you can find things to learn from your fellow group member's dream, and that the original dreamer can learn something from the whole group's participation as well.

Dream Format 8

1. Initial check in—30 minutes.

2. First dream character—Silent/Point of View or Dialoguing—5 to 15 minutes.

3. Second dream character—Partners/Dialoguing—25 to 30 per person, including sharing time; up to 60 minutes total.

4. Third dream character—Silent/Point of View or Dialoguing—5 to 15 minutes.

5. Partners/Reworking with any part of the dream—up to 15 minutes per person (30 minutes total); or Silent/Reworking—10 minutes.

6. Leader/Expanded Dream Body—20 to 25 minutes.

7. Last group sharing—30 minutes.

Dream Format 9

1. Initial check in—30 minutes.

2. First dream character—Partners/Dialoguing—25 to 30 minutes per person, including sharing time; up to one hour total; or Silent Dialoguing with all three dream characters—10 to 15 minutes per character, and 30 to 45 minutes total.

3. With whole dream—Silent/Themes—20 to 30 minutes.

4. All three dream characters—Leader/Dream Dance—20-plus minutes.

5. Last group sharing—30 minutes.

WAKING DREAM MEETING SUGGESTIONS

As I've mentioned before, you can do any of the formats above with three characters from a day in your waking life, or from a specific event in which you were involved during your waking hours. You can also try one of the formats listed below with some aspect of your waking experience, or make up your own format! (Many of the exercises that follow are found in Part Three of this book.)

Waking Format 1

1. Initial check in. Ask each person to describe a goal that they have for themselves—30 to 45 minutes.

2. Partners/Dream Dance to Help You Realize a Goal—25 to 30 minutes per person, including sharing time; up to one hour total.

3. Partners/Inner Wise Woman/Medicine Man Dialogue—25 to 30 minutes per person, including sharing time; up to one hour total. (If you have time, you could do the Dream Body exercise with your partner, using your inner wise women or medicine men as your dream characters; or you could skip the partner work and do Silent/ Wise Woman/Medicine Man Dialogue—10 to 15 minutes, followed by Leader/Dream Body—10 to 15 minutes.

4. Last group sharing—30 minutes.

Waking Format 2

1. First group sharing. Ask each person to describe both a part of her/his body that feels as though it would like some nurturing right now, and someone with whom she or he is either in conflict with or with whom she or he would like to create a deepening relationship—30 minutes.

2. Silent/Body Dream, done with Dialoguing—15 to 20 minutes.

3. Partners/Relationship Dialogue—30 to 35 minutes per person, including sharing time; up to 70 minutes total; or Silent/Relationship Dialogue—15 to 20 minutes, followed by Leader/Dream Body—10 to 15 minutes; plus note-taking time—5 minutes.

4. Partners/Your Heart Dialogue—15 to 20 minutes per person, including sharing time; up to 40 minutes total; or Silent/Heart Dialogue—15 to 20 minutes.

5. Last group sharing—30 minutes.

Waking Format 3

1. Initial check in. Ask each person to pick a food she/he would like to work with (one you are either currently

craving or one whose effect you'd like to understand more clearly). Then choose three different areas of your life you'd like to integrate more fully. Share these with the group—30 minutes.

2. Partners/Food Dialogue—15 to 20 minutes per person, including sharing time; up to 40 minutes total. Or Silent/Food Dialogue—15 to 20 minutes, possibly followed by Leader/Dream Body—10 to 15 minutes, plus note-taking—5 minutes.

3. Partners/Money Dialogue—30 minutes per person, including sharing time; up to one hour total. Or Silent/Money Dialogue—15 to 20 minutes, possibly followed by Leader/Dream Body—10 to 15 minutes, plus note-taking—5 minutes.

4. Leader/Dream Dance for Integrating Different Parts of Your Life; up to 30 minutes.

5. Last group sharing—30 minutes.

Waking Format 4

1. Initial check in. Ask each group member to describe some choice they are currently seeking to make in their lives, or that they might like or need to make before long. Share this with the group—30 minutes.

2. Partners/Dream Dance to Help You Make a Choice. In this exercise, one of you will be the Dancer and the other, the Witness. The Witness will read the exercise out loud to the Dancer and observe the Dancer's movements. When the Dancer feels complete she or he can share impressions of the experience. Then the Witness can share whatever she or he saw and felt taking place. Then reverse roles—30 to 35 minutes per person, or 70 minutes total.

3. Partners/Great Spirit Dialogue. Each of you writes down any questions you would like to ask the Great Spirit at this time. Besides specific questions, you might also want to include: How do you see me? What is it you'd like me to learn right now? Is there any way I can make my learning process easier? What can you tell me about allowing more love into my life? Is there anything else you have to tell me? Once you have written down your questions, one of you imagines that you are your own "Great Spirit," while your partner asks you to answer the questions you have written down—30 minutes per person; up to one hour total. (You can also do this one silently, for about 15 to 20 minutes.)

4. Last group sharing—30 minutes

SUMMARY

Now, you have all the tools you need to share some heartfelt dream explorations with a group of other committed people. You know how to handle the logistics, you understand what kinds of agreements it's helpful to make, and you have lots of suggestions for possible ways to put your meetings together. Be sure to change, twist, or reshape this information so it works for you—and have fun! I make some wonderfully deep connections with others when I am leading dream circles. With all my heart, I wish the same for you. May you be reminded ever so sweetly of what a wonderful experience it is to support one another in accessing and expressing your inner wisdom.

Farewell for Now

Well, here we are. This is the end and the beginning. Now is the time when you get to gather any new seeds of inspiration you have gleaned from this book and sow them in your own world in your own unique way.

I deeply hope that as you journey forth, you will remember again and again the wisdom that is so much a part of who you are . . . and so much a part of your dreams. Keep reminding yourself at all times that you are an amazing person, a magical dreamer, and a powerful channel for love. Believe in yourself.

And if ever you need reminding of your true essence, come back and visit me in these pages. Otherwise, know that I send love to your bright spirit, and I look forward to meeting you on the dream path.

The sparkling light within me honors the sparkling light within you.

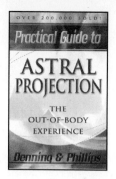

Practical Guide to Astral Projection
The Out-of-Body Experience

DENNING & PHILLIPS

Yes, your consciousness can be sent forth, out of the body, with full awareness, and return with full memory. You can travel through time and space, converse with nonphysical entities, obtain knowledge by nonmaterial means, and experience higher dimensions.

Is there life after death? Are we forever shackled by time and space? The ability to go forth by means of the astral body, or body of light, gives personal assurance of consciousness (and life) beyond the limitations of the physical body. No other answer to these ageless questions is as meaningful as experienced reality.

The reader is led through the essential stages for inner growth and development that will culminate in fully conscious projection and return. Guidance is also given to the astral world itself: what to expect, what can be done—including the ecstatic experience of astral sex between two people who project together into this higher world where true union is consummated free of the barriers of physical bodies.

978-0-87542-181-0, 216 pp., 5³⁄₁₆ x 8   **$12.95**

Inner Power

Six Techniques for Increased Energy & Self-Healing

COLLEEN DEATSMAN

Countless people worldwide are afflicted with chronic diseases for which there is no known medical cure. For ten years, Colleen Deatsman suffered from such an illness that sapped her strength, life force, and spirit. Determined to revitalize her life, she tested dozens of alternative therapies and miraculously found her way back to health.

Inner Power presents Deatsman's proven program for self-healing that ignited her remarkable recovery. It includes methods for developing self-awareness, reducing tension, clearing energy blockages, and replenishing one's life force, which helps to protect against viruses, harmful bacteria, and allergens. These powerful techniques—involving meditation, visualization, self-hypnosis, and journeying—can help readers uncover the roots of their illness and ultimately restore physical and spiritual harmony.

978-0-7387-0667-2, 336 pp., 7½ x 9⅛   **$17.95**

Lucid Dreaming for Beginners

Simple Techniques for Creating Interactive Dreams

MARK MCELROY

One third of our lives is spent asleep, passively enduring the pleasures and terrors of our dreams. What if you could take charge of your dream life and transform slumber into a fun, enriching adventure?

Step inside the exciting and gratifying world of lucid dreaming. Mark McElroy explores the stages of sleep and explains how to boost your lucid dreaming potential. Techniques for encouraging lucid dreams are punctuated by funny, enlightening anecdotes from the author and other lucid dreamers—sharing what they've learned. Once you've mastered self-awareness while dreaming, you'll be able to fly like a bird, visit loved ones who've passed on, fulfill sexual fantasies—anything you desire!

This book also explores lucid dreaming as a gateway to personal insights, astral realms, past lives, personal goals, and more.

978-0-7387-0887-4, 288 pp., 5³⁄₁₆ x 8   **$14.95**

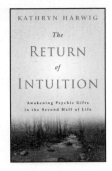

The Return of Intuition

Awakening Psychic Gifts in the Second Half of Life

KATHRYN HARWIG

Natural psychic sensitivity is often associated with children. However, The Return of Intuition reveals a little-known, widespread phenomenon of profound intuitive awakening occurring in adults—usually around the age of fifty.

Bringing this remarkable trend to light is psychic medium Kathryn Harwig, who has helped clients nationwide understand, nurture, and embrace their newfound psychic awareness. Their inspiring stories highlight what triggers this life-changing gift—usually illness or the death of a loved one—and how it can be used to aid others, receive messages from friends and family in spirit, and begin life anew with confidence, courage, and clarity. Affirming the joys of aging, this unique spiritual guide offers comfort and support to the elders of our society, encouraging them to reclaim their once-revered roles—as the crone, shaman, and sage—by passing on spiritual wisdom to a new generation.

978-0-7387-1880-4, 216 pp., 5³⁄₁₆ x 8   **$15.95**

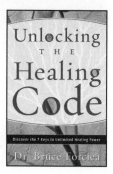

Unlocking the Healing Code
Discover the 7 Keys to Unlimited Healing Power

DR. BRUCE FORCIEA

Have you wondered why traditional medicine as well as herbs, homeopathy, and other alternative practices all work? They are all linked by a universal, mysterious field of energy that is alive with useful information. This healing information flows from the source to us across four channels, and anyone can learn how to activate these channels to heal injuries and recover from illness.

Bridging the gap between traditional and alternative health-care, Dr. Bruce Forciea introduces seven keys to unlocking this unlimited healing power. His techniques, useful for both patients and practi-tioners, help you choose and apply complementary healing methodologies—such as creative visualization, vitamins, herbs, magnets, microcurrents, light, and chiropractics. True stories, including the author's own experience with recovering from chronic illness, highlight how numerous people have found relief using this groundbreaking program for healing.

978-0-7387-1077-8, 216 pp., 6 x 9   **$14.95**